POEMS

BY

HENRY W. LONGFELLOW.

CHICAGO:

Donohue, Henneberry & Co.,

407-429 DEARBORN STREET.

CONTENTS.

———

	PAGE.
PRELUDE,	9
VOICES OF THE NIGHT,	
Hymn to the Night,	17
A Psalm of Life,	19
The Reaper and the Flowers,	21
The Light of the Stars,	23
Footsteps of Angels,	25
Flowers,	27
The Beleaguered City,	31
Midnight Mass for the Dying Year,	34
EARLIER POEMS.	
An April Day,	39
Autumn,	41
Woods in Winter,	44
Hymn of the Moravian Nuns of Bethlehem, ...	46
Sunrise on the Hills,	49
The Spirit of Poetry,	51
Burial of the Minnisink,	55
TRANSLATIONS.	
Coplas de Manrique.	61
The Good Shepherd,	84
To-morrow,	86

Contents.

PAGE.

The Native Land, ... 88
The Image of God, ... 89
The Brook, ... 90
The Celestial Pilot, ... 92
The Terrestrial Paradise, ... 95
Beatrice, ... 98
Spring, ... 101
The Child Asleep, ... 103
The Grave, ... 105
King Christian, ... 107
The Happiest Land, ... 109
The Wave, ... 111
The Dead, ... 112
The Bird and the Ship, ... 113
Whither? 115
Beware! 117
Song of the Bell, ... 119
The Castle by the Sea, ... 121
The Black Knight, ... 123
Song of the Silent Land, ... 126
L'Envoi, ... 128

BALLADS AND OTHER POEMS.

Preface, ... 131
The Skeleton in Armor, ... 145
The Wreck of the Hesperus, ... 154
The Luck of Edenhall, ... 159
The Elected Knight, ... 162
The Children of the Lord's Supper, ... 165

MISCELLANEOUS.

The Village Blacksmith, ... 195

Contents.

PAGE-

Endymion, ... 198
The Two Locks of Hair, ... 200
It is not always May, ... 202
The Rainy Day, ... 204
God's-Acre, ... 205
To the River Charles, ... 207
Blind Bartimeus, ... 209
The Goblet of Life, ... 211
Maidenhood, ... 214
Excelsior, ... 217

POEMS ON SLAVERY.

To William E. Channing, ... 223
The Slave's Dream, ... 225
The Good Part, that shall not be taken away, .. 228
The Slave in the Dismal Swamp, ... 230
The Slave singing at Midnight, ... 232
The Witness, ... 234
The Quadroon Girl, ... 236
The Warning, ... 239

PRELUDE.

PRELUDE.

Pleasant it was, when woods were green,
  And winds were soft and low,
To lie amid some sylvan scene,
Where, the long drooping boughs between,
Shadows dark and sunlight sheen
  Alternate come and go ;

Or where the denser grove receives
  No sunlight from above,
But the dark foliage interweaves
In one unbroken roof of leaves,
Underneath whose sloping eaves
  The shadows hardly move.

Beneath some patriarchal tree
  I lay upon the ground ;
His hoary arms uplifted he,
And all the broad leaves over me
Clapped their little hands in glee,
  With one continuous sound ;—

y

A slumberous sound,—a sound that **brings**
   The feelings of a dream,—
As of innumerable wings,
As when a bell no longer swings,
Faint the hollow murmur rings
   O'er meadow, lake, and stream.

And dreams of that which cannot **die,**
   Bright visions, came to me,
As lapped in thought I used to lie,
And gaze into the summer sky,
Where the sailing clouds went by,
   Like ships upon the sea ;

Dreams that the soul of youth **engage**
   Ere Fancy has been quelled ;
Old legends of the monkish page,
Traditions of the saint and sage,
Tales that have the rime of age,
   And chronicles of Eld.

And, loving still these quaint old **themes,**
   Even in the city's throng
I feel the freshness of the streams,
That, crossed by shades and sunny **gleams,**
Water the green land of dreams,
   The holy land of song.

Therefore, at Pentecost, which brings
  The Spring, clothed like a bride,
When nestling buds unfold their wings,
And bishops' caps have golden rings,
Musing upon many things,
  I sought the woodlands wide.

The green trees whispered low and mild;
  It was a sound of joy!
They were my playmates when a child,
And rocked me in their arms so wild!
Still they looked at me and smiled,
  As if I were a boy;

And ever whispered, mild and low,
  "Come, be a child once more!"
And waved their long arms to and fro,
And beckoned solemnly and slow;
O, I could not choose but go
  Into the woodlands hoar;

Into the blithe and breathing air,
  Into the solemn wood,
Solemn and silent everywhere!
Nature with folded hands seemed there,
Kneeling at her evening prayer!
  Like one in prayer I stood.

Before me rose an avenue
    Of tall and sombrous pines;
Abroad their fan-like branches grew,
And, where the sunshine darted through,
Spread a vapor soft and blue,
    In long and sloping lines.

And, falling on my weary brain,
    Like a fast-falling shower,
The dreams of youth came back again;
Low lispings of the summer rain,
Dropping on the ripened grain,
    At once upon the flower.

Visions of childhood! Stay, O stay.
    Ye were so sweet and wild!
And distant voices seemed to say,
"It cannot be! They pass away'
Other themes demand thy lay;
    Thou art no more a child!

"The land of Song within thee lies,
    Watered by living springs;
The lids of Fancy's sleepless eyes
And gates unto that Paradise,
Holy thoughts, like stars, arise,
    Its clouds are angels' wings.

"Learn, that henceforth thy song shall be,
  Not mountains capped with snow,
Nor forest sounding like the sea,
Nor rivers flowing ceaselessly,
Where the woodlands bend to see
  The bending heavens below.

"There is a forest where the din
  Of iron branches sounds !
A mighty river roars between,
And whosoever looks therein
Sees the heavens all black with sin,
Sees not its depths, nor bounds.

"Athwart the swinging branches cast
  Soft rays of sunshine pour ;
Then comes the fearful wintry blast ;
Our hopes, like withered leaves, fall fast ;
Pallid lips say, ' It is past !
  We can return no more ! '

"Look, then, into thine heart, and write !
  Yes, into Life's deep stream !
All forms of sorrow and delight,
All solemn Voices of the Night,
That can soothe thee, or affright,—
  Be these henceforth thy theme."

HYMN TO THE NIGHT.

'Ασπασίη τρίλλιστος.

I HEARD the trailing garments of the Night
    Sweep through her marble halls !
I saw her sable skirts all fringed with light
    From the celestial walls !

I felt her presence, by its spell of might,
    Stoop o'er me from above ;
The calm, majestic presence of the Night,
    As of the one I love.

I heard the sounds of sorrow and delight,
    The manifold, soft chimes,
That fill the haunted chambers of the Night,
    Like some old poet's rhymes.

From the cool cisterns of the midnight air
    My spirit drank repose ;
The fountain of perpetual peace flows
      there,—
    From those deep cisterns flows.

O holy Night ! from thee I learn to bear
  What man has borne before !
Thou layest thy finger on the lips of Care,
  And they complain no more.

Peace ! Peace ! Orestes-like I breathe this
    prayer !
  Descend with broad-winged flight,
The welcome, the thrice-prayed-for, the
    most fair,
  The best-beloved Night !

A PSALM OF LIFE.

TELL me not, in mournful numbers,
  "Life is but an empty dream!"
For the soul is dead that slumbers,
  And things are not what they seem.

Life is real! Life is earnest!
  And the grave is not its goal;
"Dust thou art, to dust returnest,"
  Was not spoken of the soul.

Not enjoyment, and not sorrow,
  Is our destined end or way;
But to act, that each to-morrow
  Find us farther than to-day.

Art is long, and Time is fleeting,
  And our hearts, though stout and brave,
Still, like muffled drums, are beating
  Funeral marches to the grave.

In the world's broad field of battle,
    In the bivouac of Life,
Be not like dumb, driven cattle!
    Be a hero in the strife!

Trust no Future, howe'er pleasant!
    Let the dead Past bury its dead!
Act,—act in the living Present!
    Heart within, and God o'erhead!

Lives of great men all remind us
    We can make our lives sublime,
And, departing, leave behind us
    Footsteps on the sands of time;

Footsteps, that perhaps another,
    Sailing o'er life's solemn main,
A forlorn and shipwrecked brother,
    Seeing, shall take heart again.

Let us, then, be up and doing,
    With a heart for any fate;
Still achieving, still pursuing,
    Learn to labor and to wait.

THE REAPER AND THE FLOWERS.

THERE is a Reaper, whose name is Death,
  And, with his sickle keen,
He reaps the bearded grain at a breath,
  And the flowers that grow between.

"Shall I have nought that is fair?" saith
    he;
  " Have nought but the bearded grain?
Though the breath of these flowers is sweet
    to me,
  I will give them all back again."

He gazed at the flowers with tearful eyes,
  He kissed their drooping leaves;
It was for the Lord of Paradise
  He bound them in his sheaves.

" My Lord has need of these flowerets gay,"
  The Reaper said, and smiled;
" Dear tokens of the earth are they,
  Where He was once a child.

21

"They shall all bloom in fields of light,
  Transplanted by my care,
And saints, upon their garments white,
  These sacred blossoms wear."

And the mother gave, in tears and pain,
  The flowers she most did love;
She knew she should find them all again
  In the fields of light above.

O, not in cruelty, not in wrath,
  The Reaper came that day;
'T was an angel visited the green earth,
  And took the flowers away.

THE LIGHT OF STARS.

THE night is come, but not too soon;
   And sinking silently,
All silently, the little moon
   Drops down behind the sky.

There is no light in earth or heaven
   But the cold light of stars;
And the first watch of night is given
   To the red planet Mars.

Is it the tender star of love?
   The star of love and dreams?
O no! from that blue tent above
   A hero's armor gleams.

And earnest thoughts within me rise,
   When I behold afar,
Suspended in the evening skies,
   The shield of that red star.

O star of strength ! I see thee stand
    And smile upon my pain ;
Thou beckonest with thy mailed hand,
    And I am strong again.

Within my breast there is no light,
    But the cold light of stars ;
I give the first watch of the night
    To the red planet Mars.

The star of the unconquered will,
    He rises in my breast,
Serene, and resolute, and still,
    And calm, and self-possessed.

And thou, too, whosoe'er thou art,
    That readest this brief psalm,
As one by one thy hopes depart,
    Be resolute and calm.

O fear not in a world like this,
    And thou shalt know ere long,
Know how sublime a thing it is
    To suffer and be strong.

FOOTSTEPS OF ANGELS.

WHEN the hours of Day are numbered,
   And the voices of the Night
Wake the better soul, that slumbered,
   To a holy, calm delight ;

Ere the evening lamps are lighted,
   And, like phantoms grim and tall,
Shadows from the fitful firelight
   Dance upon the parlor wall ;

Then the forms of the departed
   Enter at the open door ;
The beloved, the true-hearted,
   Come to visit me once more ;

He, the young and strong, who cherished
   Noble longings for the strife,
By the road-side fell and perished,
   Weary with the march of life !

25

They, the holy ones and weakly,
  Who the cross of suffering bore,
Folded their pale hands so meekly,
  Spake with us on earth no more!

And with them the Being Beauteous,
  Who unto my youth was given,
More than all things else to love me,
  And is now a saint in heaven.

With a slow and noiseless footstep
  Comes that messenger divine,
Takes the vacant chair beside me,
  Lays her gentle hand in mine.

And she sits and gazes at me
  With those deep and tender eyes,
Like the stars, so still and saint-like,
  Looking downward from the skies.

Uttered not, yet comprehended,
  Is the spirit's voiceless prayer,
Soft rebukes, in blessings ended,
  Breathing from her lips of air.

O, though oft depressed and lonely,
  All my fears are laid aside,
If I but remember only
  Such as these have lived and died!

FLOWERS.

Spake full well, in language quaint and
    olden,
  One who dwelleth by the castled Rhine,
When he called the flowers, so blue and
    golden,
  Stars, that in earth's firmament do shine.

Stars they are, wherein we read our history,
  As astrologers and seers of eld ;
Yet not wrapped about with awful mystery,
  Like the burning stars, which they beheld.

Wondrous truths, and manifold as won-
    drous,
  God hath written in those stars above ;
But not less in the bright flowerets under us
  Stands the revelation of His love.

Bright and glorious is that revelation,
  Written all over this great world of ours ;

Making evident our own creation,
   In these stars of earth,—these golden
      flowers.

And the Poet, faithful and far-seeing,
   Sees, alike in stars and flowers, a part
Of the self-same, universal being,
   Which is throbbing in his brain and heart.

Gorgeous flowerets in the sunlight shining,
   Blossoms flaunting in the eye of day,
Tremulous leaves, with soft and silver lining,
   Buds that open only to decay ;

Brilliant hopes, all woven in gorgeous
      tissues,
   Flaunting gayly in the golden light ;
Large desires, with most uncertain issues,
   Tender wishes, blossoming at night !

These in flowers and men are more than
      seeming ;
   Workings are they of the self-same powers,
Which the Poet, in no idle dreaming,
   Seeth in himself and in the flowers.

Everywhere about us are they glowing,
   Some like stars, to tell us Spring is born ;

Others, their blue eyes with tears o'erflowing,
   Stand like Ruth amid the golden corn ;

Not alone in Spring's armorial bearing,
   And in Summer's green-emblazoned field,
But in arms of brave old Autumn's wearing,
   In the center of his blazen shield ;

Not alone in meadows and green alleys,
   On the mountain-top, and by the brink
Of sequestered pools in woodland valleys,
   Where the slaves of Nature stoop to drink ;

Not alone in her vast dome of glory,
   Not on graves of bird and beast alone,
But in old cathedrals, high and hoary,
   On the tombs of heroes, carved in stone ;

In the cottage of the rudest peasant,
   In ancestral homes, whose crumbling
      towers,
Speaking of the Past unto the Present,
   Tell us of the ancient Games of Flowers ;

In all places, then, and in all seasons,
   Flowers expand their light and soul-like
      wings,

Teaching us, by most persuasive reasons,
    How akin they are to human things.

And with childlike, credulous affection
    We behold their tender buds expand ;
Emblems of our own great resurrection,
    Emblems of the bright and better land.

THE BELEAGUERED CITY.

I have read, in some old marvelous tale,
  Some legend strange and vague,
That a midnight host of spectres pale
  Beleaguered the walls of Prague.

Beside the Moldau's rushing stream,
  With the wan moon overhead,
There stood, as in an awful dream,
  The army of the dead.

White as a sea-fog, landward bound,
  The spectral camp was seen,
And, with a sorrowful, deep sound,
  The river flowed between.

No other voice nor sound was there,
  No drum, nor sentry's pace ;
The mist-like banners clasped the air,
  As clouds with clouds embrace.

But, when the old cathedral bell
　　Proclaimed the morning prayer,
The white pavilions rose and fell
　　On the alarmed air.

Down the broad valley fast and far
　　The troubled army fled ;
Up rose the glorious morning star,
　　The ghastly host was dead.

I have read, in the marvelous heart of **man,**
　　That strange and mystic scroll,
That an army of phantoms vast and **wan**
　　Beleaguer the human soul.

Encamped beside Life's rushing **stream,**
　　In Fancy's misty light,
Gigantic shapes and shadows gleam
　　Portentous through the night.

Upon its midnight battle-ground
　　The spectral camp is seen,
And, with a sorrowful, deep sound.
　　Flows the River of Life between.

No other voice nor sound is there,
　　In the army of the grave :

No other challenge breaks the air,
 But the rushing of Life's wave.

And, when the solemn and deep church-bell
 Entreats the soul to pray,
The midnight phantoms feel the spell,
 The shadows sweep away.

Down the broad Vale of Tears afar
 The spectral camp is fled ;
Faith shineth as a morning star,
 Our ghastly fears are dead.
  3

MIDNIGHT MASS FOR THE DYING YEAR.

Yes, the Year is growing old,
    And his eye is pale and bleared!
Death, with frosty hand and cold,
    Plucks the old man by the beard,
        Sorely,—sorely!

The leaves are falling, falling,
    Solemnly and slow;
" Caw! caw! " the rooks are calling,
    It is a sound of woe,
        A sound of woe!

Through woods and mountain passes
    The winds, like anthems, roll;
They are chanting solemn masses,
    Singing, " Pray for this poor soul,
        Pray,—pray! "

And the hooded clouds, like friars,
    Tell their beads in drops of rain,

34

And patter their doleful prayers ;—
  But their prayers are all in vain,
    All in vain !

There he stands in the foul weather,
  The foolish, fond Old Year,
Crowned with wild flowers and with heather,
  Like weak, despised Lear,
    A king,—a king !

Then comes the summer-like day,
  Bids the old man rejoice !
His joy ! his last ! O, the old man gray
  Loveth that ever-soft voice,
    Gentle and low.

To the crimson woods he saith,—
  To the voice gentle and low
Of the soft air, like a daughter's breath,—
  "Pray do not mock me so !
    Do not laugh at me !"

And now the sweet day is dead ;
  Cold in his arms it lies :
As stain from its breath is spread
  Over the glassy skies,
    No mist or stain !

Then, too, the Old Year dieth,
  And the forests utter a moan,
Like the voice of one who crieth
  In the wilderness alone,
    "Vex not his ghost!"

Then comes, with an awful roar,
  Gathering and sounding on,
The storm-wind from Labrador,
  The wind Euroclydon,
    The storm-wind!

Howl! howl! and from the forest
  Sweep the red leaves away!
Would, the sins that thou abhorrest,
  O Soul! could thus decay,
    And be swept away!

For there shall come a mightier blast,
  There shall be a darker day;
And the stars, from heaven down-cast,
  Like red leaves be swept away!
    Kyrie, eleyson!
    Christe, eleyson!

EARLIER POEMS.

[These poems were written for the most part during my college life, and all of them before the age of nineteen. Some have found their way into schools, and seem to be successful. Others lead a vagabond and precarious existence in the corners of newspapers; or have changed their names and run away to seek their fortunes beyond the sea. I say, with the Bishop of Avranches, on a similar occasion: " I cannot be displeased to see these children of mine, which I have neglected, and almost exposed, brought from their wanderings in lanes and alleys, and safely lodged, in order to go forth into the world together in a more decorous garb."]

AN APRIL DAY.

WHEN the warm sun, that brings
Seed-time and harvest, has returned again,
'Tis sweet to visit the still wood, where
      springs
  The first flower of the plain.

I love the season well,
When forest glades are teeming with bright
      forms,
Nor dark and many-folded clouds foretell
  The coming-on of storms.

From the earth's loosened mould
The sapling draws its sustenance, and
      thrives ;   [cold,
Though stricken to the heart with winter's
  The drooping tree revives.

The softly-warbled song
Comes from the pleasant woods, and colored
      wings

Glance quick in the bright sun, that moves
      along
    The forest openings.

When the bright sunset fills
The silver woods with light, the green slope
      throws
Its shadows in the hollows of the hills,
    And wide the upland glows.

And, when the eve is born,
In the blue lake the sky, o'er-reaching far,
Is hollowed out, and the moon dips her
      horn,
    And twinkles many a star.

Inverted in the tide,
Stand the gray rocks, and trembling shadows
      throw,
And the fair trees look over, side by side,
    And see themselves below.

Sweet April!—many a thought
Is wedded unto thee, as hearts are wed;
Nor shall they fail, till, to its autumn
      brought,
    Life's golden fruit is shed.

AUTUMN.

WITH what a glory comes and goes the
    year !
The buds of spring, those beautiful har-
    bingers
Of sunny skies and cloudless times, enjoy
Life's newness, and earth's garniture spread
    out ;
And when the silver habit of the clouds
Comes down upon the autumn sun, and
    with
A sober gladness the old year takes up
His bright inheritance of golden fruits,
A pomp and pageant fill the splendid scene.

   There is a beautiful spirit breathing now
Its mellow richness on the clustered trees,
And, from a beaker full of richest dyes,
Pouring new glory on the autumn woods,
And dipping in warm light the pillared
    clouds.

Morn on the mountain, like a summer bird,
Lifts up her purple wing, and in the vales
The gentle wind, a sweet and passionate
    wooer,
Kisses the blushing leaf, and stirs up life
Within the solemn woods of ash deep-crim-
    soned,
And silver beech, and maple yellow-leaved,
Where autumn, like a faint old man, sits
    down
By the wayside a-weary. Through the trees
The golden robin moves. The purple
    finch,
That on wild cherry and red cedar feeds,
A winter bird, comes with its plaintive
    whistle,
And pecks by the witch-hazel, whilst aloud
From cottage roofs the warbling blue-bird
    sings,
And merrily, with oft-repeated stroke,
Sounds from the threshing-floor the busy
    flail.

O what a glory doth this world put on
For him who, with a fervent heart, goes
    forth
Under the bright and glorious sky, and looks

On duties well performed, and days well
    spent!
For him the wind, ay, and the yellow
    leaves
Shall have a voice, and give him eloquent
    teachings.
He shall so hear the solemn hymn, that
    Death
He lifted up for all, that he shall go
To his long resting-place without a tear.

WOODS IN WINTER.

WHEN winter winds are piercing chill,
   And through the hawthorn blows the gale,
With solemn feet I tread the hill,
   That overbrows the lonely vale.

O'er the bare upland, and away
   Through the long reach of desert woods,
The embracing sunbeams chastely play,
   And gladden these deep solitudes.

Where, twisted round the barren oak,
   The summer vine in beauty clung,
And summer winds the stillness broke,
   The crystal icicle is hung.

Where, from their frozen urns, mute springs
   Pour out the river's gradual tide,
Shrilly the skater's iron rings,
   And voices fill the woodland side.

44

Alas ! how changed from the fair scene,
　When birds sang out their mellow lay,
And winds were soft, and woods were green
　And the song ceased not with the day.

But still wild music is abroad,
　Pale, desert woods ! within your crowd ;
And gathering winds, in hoarse accord,
　Amid the vocal reeds pipe loud.

Chill airs and wintry winds ! my ear
　Has grown familiar with your song ;
I hear it in the opening year,—
　I listen, and it cheers me long.

HYMN OF THE MORAVIAN NUNS OF BETHLEHEM

AT THE CONSECRATION OF PULASKI'S BANNER.

WHEN the dying flame of day
Through the chancel shot its ray,
Far the glimmering tapers shed
Faint light on the cowled head ;
And the censer burning swung,
Where, before the altar, hung
The blood-red banner, that with prayer
Had been consecrated there.

And the nuns' sweet hymn was heard the
    while,
Sung low in the dim, mysterious aisle.

"Take thy banner ! May it wave
    Proudly o'er the good and brave ;
    When the battle's distant wail
    Breaks the Sabbath of our vale,
    46

When the clarion's music thrills
To the hearts of these lone hills,
When the spear in conflict shakes,
And the strong lance shivering breaks.

"Take thy banner! and, beneath
The battle-cloud's encircling wreath,
Guard it!—till our homes are free!
Guard it!—God will prosper thee!
In the dark and trying hour,
In the breaking forth of power,
In the rush of steeds and men,
His right hand will shield thee then.

"Take thy banner! But, when night
Closes round the ghastly fight,
If the vanquished warrior bow,
Spare him!—By our holy vow,
By our prayers and many tears,
By the mercy that endears,
Spare him!—he our love hath shared!
Spare him!—as thou wouldst be spared!

"Take thy banner!—and if e'er
Thou shouldst press the soldier's bier,
And the muffled drum should beat
To the tread of mournful feet,

Then this crimson flag shall be
Martial cloak and shroud for thee."

The warrior took that banner proud,
And it was his martial cloak and shroud!

SUNRISE ON THE HILLS.

I stood upon the hills, when heaven's wide
    arch
Was glorious with the sun's returning march,
And woods were brightened, and soft gales
Went forth to kiss the sun-clad vales.
The clouds were far beneath me ;—bathed
    in light,
They gathered mid-way round the wooded
    height,
And, in their fading glory, shone
Like hosts in battle overthrown,
As many a pinnacle, with shifting glance,
Through the gray mist thrust up its shattered
    lance,
And rocking on the cliff was left
The dark pine blasted, bare, and cleft.
The veil of cloud was lifted, and below
Glowed the rich valley, and the river's flow
Was darkened by the forest's shade,
Or glistened in the white cascade ;

Where upward, in the mellow blush of day,
The noisy bittern wheeled his spiral way.

I heard the distant waters dash,
I saw the current whirl and flash,—
And richly, by the blue lake's silver beach,
The woods were bending with a silent reach.
Then o'er the vale, with gentle swell,
The music of the village bell
Came sweetly to the echo-giving hills ;
And the wild horn, whose voice the wood-
    land fills,
Was ringing to the merry shout,
That faint and far the glen sent out,
Where, answering to the sudden shot, thin
    smoke,
Through thick-leaved branches, from the
    dingle broke.

If thou art worn and hard beset
With sorrows, that thou wouldst forget,
If thou wouldst read a lesson, that will keep
Thy heart from fainting and thy soul from
    sleep,
Go to the woods and hills !—No tears
Dim the sweet look that Nature wears.

THE SPIRIT OF POETRY.

There is a quiet spirit in these woods,
That dwell's where'er the gentle south wind
    blows ;
Where, underneath the white-thorn, in the
    glade,
The wild flowers bloom, or, kissing the soft
    air,
The leaves above their sunny palms out-
    spread.
With what a tender and impassioned voice
It fills the nice and delicate ear of thought,
When the fast-ushering star of morning
    comes
O'er-riding the gray hills with golden scarf ;
Or when the cowled and dusky-sandaled
    Eve,
In mourning weeds, from out the western
    gate,
Departs with silent pace !   That spirit moves
In the green valley, where the silver brook,

From its full laver, pours the wide cascade ;
And, babbling low amid the tangled woods,
Slip down through moss-grown stones with
      endless laughter.
And frequent, on the everlasting hills,
Its feet go forth, when it doth wrap itself
In all the dark embroidery of the storm,
And shouts the stern, strong wind. **And**
      here, amid
The silent majesty of these deep woods,
Its presence shall uplift thy thoughts from
      earth,
As to the sunshine and the pure, bright air
Their tops the green trees lift. Hence gifted
      bards
Have ever loved the calm and quiet shades.
For them there was an eloquent voice in
      all
The sylvan pomp of woods, the golden sun,
The flowers, the leaves, the river on its way,
Blue skies, and silver clouds, and gentle
      winds,—
The swelling upland, where the sidelong
      sun
Aslant the wooded slop, at evening, goes,—
Groves, through whose broken roof the sky
      looks in,

Mountain, and shattered cliff, and sunny
     vale.
The distant lake, fountains,—and mighty
     trees,
In many a lazy syllable, repeating
Their old poetic legends to the wind.

   And this is the sweet spirit, that doth fill
The world ; and, in these wayward days of
     youth,
My busy fancy oft embodies it,
As a bright image of the light and beauty
That dwell in nature,—of the heavenly
     forms
We worship in our dreams, and the soft hues
That stain the wild bird's wing, and flush
     the clouds
When the sun sets.   Within her eye
The heaven of April, with its changing light
And when it wears the blue of May, is hung,
And on her lip the rich, red rose.   Her hair
Is like the summer tresses of the trees,
When twilight makes them brown, and on
     her cheek
Blushes the richness of an autumn sky,
With ever-shifting beauty.   Then her breath,
It is so like the gentle air of Spring,

As, from the morning's dewy flowers, it
    comes
Full of their fragrance, that it is a joy
To have it round us,—and her silver voice
Is the rich music of a summer bird,
Heard in the still night with its passionate
    cadence.

BURIAL OF THE MINNISINK.

On sunny slope and beechen swell,
The shadowed light of evening fell ;
And, where the maple's leaf was brown,
With soft and silent lapse came down
The glory, that the wood receives,
At sunset, in its brazen leaves.

Far upward in the mellow light
Rose the blue hills.   One cloud of white
Around a fair uplifted cone,
In the warm blush of evening shone ;
An image of the silver lakes,
By which the Indian's soul awakes.

But soon a funeral hymn was heard
Where the soft breath of evening stirred
The tall, gray forest ; and a band
Of stern in heart, and strong in hand,
Came winding down beside the wave,
To lay the red chief in his grave.

They sang, that by his native bowers
He stood, in the last moon of flowers,
And thirty snows had not yet shed
Their glory on the warrior's head ;
But, as the summer fruit decays,
So died he in those naked days.

A dark cloak of the roebuck's skin
Covered the warrior, and within
Its heavy folds the weapons, made
For the hard toils of war, were laid ;
The cuirass, woven of plaited reeds,
And the broad belt of shells and beads.

Before, a dark-haired virgin train
Chanted the death dirge of the slain ;
Behind, the long procession came
Of hoary men and chiefs of fame,
With heavy hearts, and eyes of grief,
Leading the war-horse of their chief.

Stripped of his proud and martial dress
Uncurbed, unreined, and riderless,
With darting eye, and nostril spread.
And heavy and impatient tread,
He came ; and oft that eye so proud
Asked for his rider in the crowd.

They buried the dark chief ; they freed
Beside the grave his battle steed ;
And swift an arrow cleaved its way
To his stern heart !   One piercing neigh
Arose,—and, on the dead man's plain,
The rider grasps his steed again.

TRANSLATIONS.

[Don Jorge Manrique, the author of the follow-
ing poem, flourished in the last half of the
fifteenth century. He followed the profes-
sion of arms, and died on the field of
battle. Mariana, in his History of Spain,
makes honorable mention of him, as being
present at the siege of Uclés; and speaks of
him as "a youth of estimable qualities, who
in this war gave brilliant proofs of his valor.
He died young; and was thus cut off from
long exercising his great virtues, and exhib-
iting to the world the light of his genius,
which was already known to fame." He was
mortally wounded in a skirmish near Cana-
vete, in the year 1479.

The name of Rodrigo Manrique, the
father of the poet, Conde de Paredes and
Maestre de Santiago, is well known in
Spanish history and song. He died in 1476;
according to Mariana, in the town of Uclés;
but, according to the poem of his son, in
Ocana. It was his death that called forth
the poem upon which rests the literary
reputation of the younger Manrique. In the
language of his historian, "Don Jorge Man-
rique, in an elegant Ode, full of poetic beau-
ties, rich embellishments of genius, and high
moral reflections, mourned the death of his
father as with a funeral hymn." This praise
is not exaggerated. The poem is a model
in its kind. Its conception is solemn and
beautiful; and, in accordance with it, the
style moves on—calm, dignified and majes-
tic.]

60

COPLAS DE MANRIQUE.

FROM THE SPANISH.

O LET the soul her slumbers break,
Let thought be quickened, and awake ;
Awake to see
How soon this life is past and gone,
And death comes softly stealing on,
How silently !

Swiftly our pleasures glide away,
Our hearts recall the distant day
With many sighs ;
The moments that are speeding fast
We heed not, but the past,—the past,—
More highly prize.

Onward its course the present keeps,
Onward the constant current sweeps,
Till life is done ;
And, did we judge of time aright,
The past and future in their flight
Would be as one.

Let no one fondly dream again,
That Hope and all her shadowy train
Will not decay ;
Fleeting as were the dreams of old,
Remembered like a tale that's told
They pass away.

Our lives are rivers, gliding free
To that unfathomed, boundless sea,
The silent grave !
Thither all earthly pomp and boast
Roll, to be swallowed up and lost
In one dark wave.

Thither the mighty torrents stray,
Thither the brook pursues its way,
And tinkling rill.
There all are equal.   Side by side
The poor man and the son of pride
Lie calm and still.

I will not here invoke the throng
Of orators and sons of songs,
The deathless few ;
Fiction entices and deceives,
And, sprinkled o'er her fragrant leaves,
Lies poisonous dew.

To One alone my thoughts arise,
The Eternal Truth,—the Good and Wise—
To Him I cry,
Who shared on earth our common lot,
But the world comprehended not
His deity.

This world is but the rugged road
Which leads us to the bright abode
Of peace above;
So let us choose that narrow way
Which leads no traveler's foot astray
From realms of love.

Our cradle is the starting-place,
In life we run the onward race,
And reach the goal;
When, in the mansions of the blest,
Death leaves to its eternal rest
The weary soul.

Did we but use it as we ought,
This world would school each wandering
    thought
To its high state.
Faith wings the soul beyond the sky,
Up to that better world on high,
For which we wait.

Yes,—the glad messenger of love,
To guide us to our home above,
    The Saviour came;
Born amid mortal cares and fears,
He suffered in this vale of tears
    A death of shame.

Behold of what delusive worth
The bubbles we pursue on earth,
    The shapes we chase,
Amid a world of treachery !
They vanish ere death shuts the eye,
    And leave no trace.

Time steals them from us,—chances strange
Disastrous accidents, and change,
    That come to all ;
Even in the most exalted state,
Relentless sweeps the stroke of fate ;
    The strongest fall.

Tell me,—the charms that lovers seek
In the clear eye and blushing cheek,
    The hues that play
O'er rosy lip and brow of snow,
When hoary age approaches slow,
    Ah, where are they ?

The cunning skill, the curious arts,
The glorious strength that youth imparts
In life's first stage ;
These shall become a heavy weight,
When Time swings wide his outward gate
To weary age.

The noble blood of Gothic name,
Heroes emblazoned high to fame,
In long array ;
How, in the onward course of time,
The landmarks of that race sublime
Were swept away !

Some, the degraded slaves of lust,
Prostrate and trampled in the dust,
Shall rise no more ;
Others, by guilt and crime, maintain
The scutcheon, that, without a stain,
Their fathers bore.

Wealth and high estate of pride,
With what untimely speed they glide,
How soon depart !
Did not the shadowy phantoms stay,
The vassals of a mistress they,
Of fickle heart.

5

These gifts in Fortune's hands are found;
Her swift revolving wheel turns round
And they are gone !
No rest the inconstant goddess knows,
But changing, and without repose,
Still hurries on.

Even could the hand of avarice save
Its gilded baubles, till the grave
Reclaimed its prey,
Let none on such poor hopes rely ;
Life, like an empty dream, flits by,
And where are they ?

Earthly desires and sensual lust
Are passions springing from the dust, –
They fade and die ;
But, in the life beyond the tomb,
They seal the immortal spirit's doom
Eternally !

The pleasures and delights, which mask
In treacherous smiles life's serious task,
What are they, all,
But the fleet coursers of the chase
And death an ambush in the race,
Wherein we fall ?

No foe, no dangerous pass, we heed,
Brook no delay,—but onward speed
With loosened rein ;
And, when the fatal snare is near,
We strive to check our mad career,
But strive in vain.

Could we new charms to age impart,
And fashion with a cunning art
The human face,
As we can clothe the soul with light,
And make the glorious spirit bright
With heavenly grace,—

How busily each passing hour
Should we exert that magic power !
What ardor show,
To deck the sensual slave of sin,
Yes leave the freeborn soul within,
In weeds of woe !

Monarchs, the powerful and the strong
Famous in history and in song
Of olden time,
Saw, by the stern decrees of fate,
Their kingdoms lost, and desolate
Their race sublime.

Who is the champion? who the strong?
Pontiff and priest, and sceptred throng?
On these shall fall
As heavily the hand of Death,
As when it stays the shepherd's breath
Beside his stall.

I speak not of the Trojan name,
Neither its glory nor its shame
Has met our eyes;
Nor of Rome's great and glorious dead,
Though we have heard so oft, and read,
Their histories.

Little avails it now to know
Of ages passed so long ago,
Nor how they rolled;
Our theme shall be of yesterday,
Which to oblivion sweeps away,
Like days of old.

Where is the King, Don Juan? Where
Each royal prince and noble heir
Of Aragon?
Where are the courtly gallantries?
The deeds of love and high emprise,
In battle done?

Tourney and joust, that charmed the eye,
And scarf, and gorgeous panoply,
And nodding plume,—
What were they but a pageant scene,
What but the garlands, gay and green,
That deck the tomb?

Where are the high-born dames, and where
Their gay attire, and jeweled hair,
And odors sweet?
Where are the gentle knights, that came
To kneel, and breathe love's ardent flame,
Low at their feet?

Where is the song of Troubadour?
Where are the lute and gay tambour
They loved of yore?
Where is the mazy dance of old,
The flowing robes, inwrought with gold,
The dancers wore?

And he who next the sceptre swayed,
Henry, whose royal court displayed
Such power and pride;
O, in what winning smiles arrayed,
The world its various pleasures laid
His throne beside!

But O! how false and full of guile
That world, which wore so soft a smile
But to betray!
She, that had been his friend before,
Now from the fated monarch tore
Her charms away.

The countless gifts,—the stately walls,
The royal palaces, and halls
All filled with gold;
Plate with armorial bearings wrought,
Chambers with ample treasures fraught
Of wealth untold;

The noble steeds, and harness bright,
And gallant lord, and stalwart knight,
In rich array,—
Where shall we seek them now? Alas!
Like the bright dewdrops on the grass,
They passed away.

His brother, too, whose factious zeal
Usurped the sceptre of Castile,
Unskilled to reign;
What a gay, brilliant court had he,
When all the flower of chivalry
Was in his train!

But he was mortal ; and the breath,
That flamed from the hot forge of Death,
Blasted his years ;
Judgment of God ! that flame by thee,
When raging fierce and fearfully,
Was quenched in tears !

Spain's haughty Constable,—the great
And gallant Master,—cruel fate
Stripped him of all.
Breathe not a whisper of his pride,—
He on the gloomy scaffold died,
Ignoble fall !

The countless treasures of his care,
Hamlets and villas green and fair,
His mighty power,—
What were they all, but grief and shame,
Tears and a broken heart, when came
The parting hour ?

His other brothers, proud and high,
Masters, who, in prosperity,
Might rival kings ;
Who made the bravest and the best
The bondsmen of their high behest,
Their underlings ;

What was their prosperous estate.
When high exalted and elate
With power and pride?
What, but a transient gleam of light,
A flame, which, glaring at its height,
Grew dim and died?

So many a duke of royal name,
Marquis and count of spotless fame,
And baron brave,
That might the sword of empire wield,
All these, O Death, hast thou concealed
In the dark grave!

Their deeds of mercy and of arms,
In peaceful days, or war's alarms,
When thou dost show,
O Death, thy stern and angry face,
One stroke of thy all-powerful mace
Can overthrow.

Unnumbered hosts, that threaten nigh,
Pennon and standard flaunting high,
And flag displayed;
High battlements intrenched around,
Bastion, and moated wall, and mound,
And palisade,

And covered trench, secure and deep,—
All these cannot one victim keep,
O Death, from thee,
When thou dost battle in thy wrath,
And thy strong shafts pursue their **path**
Unerringly.

O World! so few the years we live,
Would that the life which thou dost **give**
Were life indeed!
Alas! thy sorows fall so fast,
Our happiest hour is when at last
The soul is freed.

Our days are covered o'er with grief,
And sorrows neither few nor brief
Veil all in gloom;
Left desolate of real good,
Within this cheerless solitude
No pleasures bloom.

Thy pilgrimage begins in tears,
And ends in bitter doubts and fears,
Or dark despair;
Midway so many toils appear,
That he who lingers longest here
Knows most of care.

Thy goods are bought with many a groan,
By the hot sweat of toil alone,
And weary hearts ;
Fleet-footed is the approach of woe,
But with a lingering step and slow
Its form departs.

And he, the good man's shield and shade,
To whom all hearts their homage paid,
As Virtue's son, —
Roderic Manrique, — he whose name
Is written on the scroll of Fame,
Spain's champion ;

His signal deeds and powers high
Demand no pompous eulogy, —
Ye saw his deeds !
Why should their praise in verse be sung?
The name, that dwells on every tongue,
No minstrel needs.

To friends a friend ; how kind to all
The vassals of this ancient hall
And feudal fief !
To foes how stern a foe was he !
And to the valiant and the free
How brave a chief !

What prudence with the old and **wise ;**
What grace in youthful gayeties ;
In all how sage !
Benignant to the serf and slave,
He showed the base and falsely **brave**
A lion's rage.

His was Octavian's prosperous star,
The rush of Cæsar's conquering **car**
At battle's call ;
His, Scipio's virtue ; his, the **skill**
And the indomitable will
Of Hannibal.

His was a Trajan's goodness,—**his**
A Titus' noble charities
And righteous laws ;
The arm of Hector, and the **might**
Of Tully, to maintain the **right**
In truth's just cause ;

The clemency of Antonine,
Aurelius' countenance divine,
Firm, gentle, still ;
The eloquence of Adrian,
And Theodosius' love to **man,**
And generous will ;

In tented field and bloody fray,
An Alexander's vigorous sway
And stern command ;
The faith of Constantine ; ay, more,
The fervent love Camillus bore
His native land.

He left no well-filled treasury,
He heaped no pile of riches high,
Nor massive plate ;
He fought the Moors,—and, in their fall,
Villa and tower and castled wall
Were his estate.

Upon the hard-fought battle-ground,
Brave steeds and gallant riders found
A common grave ;
And there the warrior's hand did gain
The rents, and the long vassal train,
The conquered gave.

And if, of old, his halls displayed
The honored and exalted grade
His worth had gained,
So, in the dark, disastrous hour,
Brothers and bondsmen of his power
His hand sustained.

After high deeds, not left untold,
In the stern warfare, which of old
'T was his to share,
Such noble leagues he made, that more
And fairer regions, than before,
His guerdon were.

These are the records, half effaced,
Which, with the hand of youth, he traced
On history's page;
But with fresh victories he drew
Each fading character anew
In his old age.

By his unrivaled skill, by great
And veteran service to the state,
By worth adored,
He stood, in his high dignity,
The proudest knight of chivalry,
Knight of the Sword.

He found his villas and domains
Beneath a tyrant's galling chains
And cruel power;
But, by fierce battle and blockade,
Soon his own banner was displayed
From every tower.

By the tried valor of his hand,
His monarch and his native **land**
Were nobly served ;—
Let Portugal repeat the story,
And proud Castile, who shared **the glory**
His arms deserved.

And when so oft, for weal or woe,
His life upon the fatal throw
Had been cast down ;
When he had served, with patriot **zeal,**
Beneath the banner of Castile,
His sovereign's crown ;

And done such deeds of valor **strong,**
That neither history nor song
Can count them all ;
Then, on Ocana's castled rock,
Death at his portal came to **knock,**
With sudden call,—

Saying, "Good Cavalier, prepare
To leave this world of toil and **care**
With joyful mien ;
Let thy strong heart of steel this **day**
Put on its armor for the fray,—
The closing scene.

" Since thou hast been, in battle-strife,
So prodigal of health and life,
    For earthly fame,
Let virtue nerve thy heart again ;
Loud on the last stern battle-plain
    They call thy name.

"Think not the struggle that draws near
Too terrible for man,—nor fear
    To meet the foe ;
Nor let thy noble spirit grieve,
Its life of glorious fame to leave
    On earth below.

" A life of honor and of worth
Has no eternity on earth,—
    'T is but a name ;
And yet its glory far exceeds
That base and sensual life, which leads
    To want and shame.

"The eternal life, beyond the sky,
Wealth cannot purchase, nor the high
    And proud estate ;
The soul in dalliance laid,—the spirit
Corrupt with sin,—shall not inherit
    A joy so great.

"But the good monk, in cloistered cell,
Shall gain it by his book and bell,
His prayers and tears ;
And the brave knight, whose arm endures
fierce battle, and against the Moors
His standard rears.

"And thou, brave knight, whose hand hast
     poured
The life-blood of the Pagan horde
O'er all the land,
In heaven shalt thou receive, at length,
The guerdon of thine earthly strength
And dauntless hand.

"Cheered onward by his promise sure,
Strong in the faith entire and pure
Thou dost profess,
Depart,—thy hope is certainty,—
The third—the better life on high
Shalt thou possess."

"O Death, no more, no more delay,
My spirit longs to flee away,
And be at rest ;
The will of Heaven my will shall be,—
I bow to the divine decree,
To God's behest.

"My soul is ready to depart,
No thought rebels, the obedient **heart**
Breathes forth no sigh;
The wish on earth to linger still
Were vain, when 't is God's sovereign **will**
That we shall die.

"O thou, that for our sins didst **take**
A human form, and humbly make
Thy home on earth;
Thou, that to thy divinity
A human nature didst ally
By mortal birth,

"And in that form didst suffer **here**
Torment, and agony, and fear,
So patiently;
By thy redeeming grace alone,
And not for merits of my own,
O, pardon me!"

As thus the dying warrior prayed,
Without one gathering mist or **shade**
Upon his mind;
Encircled by his family,
Watched by affection's **gentle eye**
So soft and kind;

6

His soul to Him who gave it rose ;
God lead it to its long repose,
Its glorious rest !
And, though the warrior's sun has set,
Its light shall linger round us yet,
Bright, radiant, blest.*

* This poem of Manrique is a great favorite in Spain.
No less than four poetic Glosses, or running commen-
taries, upon it have been published, no one of which,
however, possesses great poetic merit. That of the
Carthusian monk, Rodrigo de Valdepenas, is the best.
It is known as the *Glosa del Cartujo.* There is also a
prose Commentary by Luis de Aranda.

"O World ! so few the years we live,
     Would that the life which thou dost give
     Were life indeed !
     Alas ! thy sorrows fall so fast,
     Our happiest hour is when at last
     The soul is freed.

"Our days are covered o'er with grief,
     And sorrows neither few nor brief
     Veil all in gloom ;
     Left desolate of real good,
     Within this cheerless solitude
     No pleasures bloom.

The following stanzas of the poem were found in the
author's pocket, after his death on the field of b...

"Thy pilgrimage begins in tears
    And ends in bitter doubts and fears,
        Or dark despair;
    Midway so many toils appear,
    That he who lingers longest here
        Knows most of care.

"Thy goods are bought with many a groan,
    By the hot sweat of toil alone,
        And weary hearts;
    Fleet-footed is the approach of woe,
    But with a lingering step and slow
        Its form departs."

THE GOOD SHEPHERD.

FROM THE SPANISH OF LOPE DE VEGA.

SHEPHERD! that with thine amorous, sylvan
    song
Hast broken the slumber which encom-
    passed me, —
That mad'st thy crook from the accursed
    tree,
On which thy powerful arms were stretched
    so long!
Lead me to mercy's ever-flowing fountains;
For thou my shepherd, guard, and guide
    shalt be;
I will obey thy voice, and wait to see
Thy feet all beautiful upon the mountains.

Hear, Shepherd!—thou who for thy flock
    art dying.
O, wash away these scarlet sins, for thou
Rejoicest at the contrite sinner's vow.

84

O, wait !—to thee my weary soul is cry-
    ing,—
Wait for me !—Yet why ask it, when I see,
With feet nailed to the cross, thou 'rt wait-
    ing still for me !

TO-MORROW.

FROM THE SPANISH OF LOPE DE VEGA.

LORD, what am I, that, with unceasing
  care,
Thou didst seek after me,—that thou didst
  wait,
Wet with unhealthy dews, before my gate,
And pass the gloomy nights of winter
  there?
O strange delusion!—that I did not greet
Thy blest approach, and O, to Heaven how
  lost,
If my ingratitude's unkindly frost
Has chilled the bleeding wounds upon thy
  feet.
How oft my guardian angel gently cried,
"Soul, from thy casement look, and thou
  shalt see
How he persists to knock and wait for thee!"

And, O ! how often to that voice of sorrow,
 "To-morrow we will open," I replied,
And when the morrow came I answered
 still, "To-morrow."

THE NATIVE LAND.

FROM THE SPANISH OF FRANCISCO DE ALDANA.

CLEAR fount of light ! my native land on
    high,
Bright with a glory that shall never fade !
Mansion of truth ! without a veil or shade,
Thy holy quiet meets the spirit's eye.
There dwells the soul in its ethereal essence,
Gasping no longer for life's feeble breath ;
But, sentineled in heaven, its glorious pres-
    ence
With pitying eye beholds, yet fears not,
    death.
Beloved country ! banished from thy shore,
A stranger in this prison-house of clay,
The exiled spirit weeps and sighs for thee !
Heavenward the bright perfections I adore
Direct, and the sure promise cheers the
    way,
That, whither love aspires, there shall my
    dwelling be.

THE IMAGE OF GOD.

FROM THE SPANISH OF FRANCISCO DE ALDANA.

O LORD ! that seest, from yon starry height,
Centred in one the future and the past,
Fashioned in thine own image, see how fast
The world obscures in me what once was
    bright !
Eternal Sun ! the warmth which thou hast
    given,
To cheer life's flowery April, fast decays ;
Yet, in the hoary winter of my days,
Forever green shall be my trust in Heaven.
Celestial King ! O let thy presence pass
Before my spirit, and an image fair
Shall meet that look of mercy from on high,
As the reflected image in a glass
Doth meet the look of him who seeks it
    there,
And owes its being to the gazer's eye.

THE BROOK.

FROM THE SPANISH.

Laugh of the mountain!—lyre of bird and
 tree!
Pomp of the meadow! mirror of the morn!
The soul of April, unto whom are born
The rose and jessamine. leaps wild in
 thee!
Although, where'er thy devious current
 strays,
The lap of earth with gold and silver teems,
To me thy clear proceeding brighter seems
Than golden sands, that charm each shep-
 herd's gaze.
How without guile thy bosom, all trans-
 parent
As the pure crystal, lets the curious eye
Thy secrets scan, thy smooth, round pebbles
 count!

How, without malice, murmuring glides thy
    current !
O sweet simplicity of days gone by !
Thou shun'st the haunts of man, to dwell
    in limpid fount !

THE CELESTIAL PILOT.

FROM DANTE. PURGATORIO, II.

AND now, behold! as at the approach of
    morning,
Through the gross vapors, Mars grows fiery
    red
Down in the west upon the ocean floor,

Appeared to me,—would I again could see
    it !—
A light along the sea, so swiftly coming,
Its motion by no flight of wing is equaled,

And when therefrom I had withdrawn a little
Mine eyes, that I might question my con-
    ductor,
Again I saw it brighter grown and larger.

Thereafter, on all sides of it, appeared
I knew not what of white, and underneath,
Little by little, there came forth another.

9²

My master yet had uttered not a word,
While the first brightness into wings un-
    folded ;
But, when he clearly recognized the pilot,

He cried aloud : "Quick, quick, and bow
    the knee !
Behold the Angel of God ! fold up thy
    hands !
Henceforward shalt thou see such officers !

"See, how he scorns all human arguments,
So that no oar he wants, nor other sail
Than his own wings, between so distant
    shores !

"See, how he holds them, pointed straight
    to heaven,
Fanning the air with the eternal pinions,
That do not moult themselves like mortal
    hair !"

And then, as nearer and more near us came
The Bird of Heaven, more glorious he ap-
    peared,
So that the eye could not sustain his presence,

But down I cast it; and he came to shore
With a small vessel, gliding swift and light,
So that the water swallowed nought thereof.

Upon the stern stood the Celestial Pilot!
Beatitude seemed written in his face!
And more than a hundred spirits sat within.

" *In exitu Israel* out of Egypt!"
Thus sang they all together in one voice,
With whatso in that Psalm is after written.

Then made he sign of holy rood upon them,
Whereat all cast themselves upon the shore,
And he departed swiftly as he came.

THE TERRESTRIAL PARADISE.

FROM DANTE.   PURGATORIO, XXVIII.

Longing already to search in and round
The heavenly forest, dense and living-green,
Which to the eyes tempered the new-born
     day,

Withouten more delay I left the bank,
Crossing the level country slowly, slowly,
Over the soil, that everywhere breathed
     fragrance.

A gently-breathing air, that no mutation
Had in itself, smote me upon the forehead,
No heavier blow, than of a pleasant breeze,

Whereat the tremulous branches readily
Did all of them bow downward towards that
     side
Where its first shadow casts the Holy Moun-
     tain ;

95

Yet not from their upright direction bent
So that the little birds upon their tops
Should cease the practice of their tuneful art ;

But, with full-throated joy, the hours of
    prime
Singing received they in the midst of foliage
That made monotonous burden to their
    rhymes,

Even as from branch to branch it gathering
    swells,
Through the pine forests on the shore of
    Chiassi,
When Æolus unlooses the Sirocco.

Already my slow steps had led me on
Into the ancient wood so far, that I
Could see no more the place where I had
    entered.

And lo ! my farther course cut off a river,
Which, towards the left hand, with its little
    waves,
Bent down the grass, that on its margin
    sprang.

All waters that on earth most limpid are
Would seem to have within themselves some
     mixture,
Compared with that, which nothing doth
     conceal,

Although it moves on with a brown, brown
    current,
Under the shade perpetual, that never
Ray of the sun lets in, nor of the moon.
    7

BEATRICE.

FROM DANTE.   PURGATORIO, XXX., XXXI.

EVEN as the Blessed, in the new covenant,
Shall rise up quickened, each one from his
    grave,
Wearing again the garments of the flesh,

So, upon that celestial chariot,
A hundred rose *ad vocem tanti senis*,
Ministers and messengers of life eternal.

They all were saying,   *Benedictus qui*
    venis,"
And scattering flowers above and round
    about,
" *Manibus o date lilia plenis.*"

I once beheld, at the approach of day,
The orient sky all stained with roseate hues
And the other heaven with light serene
    adorned,
98

And the sun's face uprising, overshadowed,
So that, by temperate influence of vapors,
The eye sustained his aspect for long while ;

Thus in the bosom of a cloud of flowers,
Which from those hands angelic were thrown
    up,
And down descended inside and without,

With crown of olive o'er a snow-white veil,
Appeared a lady, under a green mantle,
Vested in colors of the living flame.

       *   *   *   *   *

Even as the snow, among the living rafters
Upon the back of Italy, congeals,
Blown on and beaten by Sclavonian winds,

And then dissolving, filters through itself,
Whene'er the land, that loses shadow,
    breathes.
Like as a taper melts before a fire,

Even such I was, without a sigh or tear,
Before the song of those who chime forever
After the chiming of the eternal spheres ;

But, when I heard in those sweet melodies
Compassion for me, more than had they said,
"O wherefore, lady, dost thou thus con-
    sume him?"

The ice, that was about my heart congealed,
To air and water changed, and in my
    anguish,
Through lips and eyes came gushing from
    my breast.

      *   *   *   *   *

Confusion and dismay, together mingled,
Forced such a feeble "Yes!" out of my
    mouth,
To understand it one had need of sight

Even as a cross-bow breaks, when 'tis dis-
    charged,
Too tensely drawn the bow-string and the
    bow,
And with less force the arrow hits the mark;

So I gave way under this heavy burden,
Gushing forth into bitter tears and sighs,
And the voice, fainting, flagged upon its
    passage.

SPRING.

FROM THE FRENCH OF CHARLES D'ORLEANS.
XV. CENTURY.

GENTLE Spring !—in sunshine clad,
  Well dost thou thy power display !
For winter maketh the light heart sad,
  And thou,—thou makest the sad heart gay.
He sees thee, and calls to his gloomy train,
The sleet, and the snow, and the wind, and
    the rain ;
And they shrink away, and they flee in fear,
  When thy merry step draws near.

Winter giveth the fields and the trees, so old,
  Their beards of icicles and snow ;
And the rain, it raineth so fast and cold,
  We must cower over the embers low ;
And, snugly housed from the wind and
    weather,
Mope like birds that are changing feather.

But the storm retires, and the sky grows
        clear,
    When thy merry step draws near.

Winter maketh the sun in the gloomy sky
    Wrap him round with a mantle of cloud ;
But, Heaven be praised, thy step is nigh ;
    Thou tearest away the mournful shroud,
And the earth looks bright and Winter surly,
Who has toiled for nought both late and
        early,
Is banished afar by the new-born year,
    When thy merry step draws near.

THE CHILD ASLEEP.

FROM THE FRENCH.

SWEET babe ! true portrait of thy father's
face,
   Sleep on the bosom, that thy lips have
     pressed !
Sleep, little one ; and closely, gently place
   Thy drowsy eyelids on thy mother's
     breast.

Upon that tender eye, my little friend,
   Soft sleep shall come, that cometh not to
     me !
I watch to see thee, nourish thee, defend ;—
   'Tis sweet to watch for thee,—alone for
     thee !

His arms fall down ; sleep sits upon his
   brow ;
   His eye is closed ; he sleeps, nor dreams
     of harm.

103

Wore not his cheek the apple's ruddy glow,
  Would you not say he slept on Death's
    cold arm?

Awake, my boy!—I tremble with affright!
  Awake, and chase this fatal thought!—
    Unclose
Thine eye but for one moment on the light!
  Even at the price of thine, give me repose!

Sweet   error!—he but slept,—I breathe
      again;—
Come, gentle dreams, the hour of sleep
      beguile!
O, when shall he, for whom I sigh in vain,
  Beside me watch to see thy waking smile?

THE GRAVE.

FROM THE ANGLO-SAXON.

For thee was a house built
Ere thou wert born,
For thee was a mould meant
Ere thou of mother camest.
But it is not made ready,
Nor its depth measured,
Nor is it seen
How long it shall be.
Now I bring thee
Where thou shall be ;
Now I shalt measure thee,
And the mould afterwards.

Thy house is not
Highly timbered,
It is unhigh and low ;
When thou art therein,
The heel-ways are low,
The side-ways unhigh.

The roof is built
Thy breast full nigh,
So thou shalt in mould
Dwell full cold,
Dimly and dark.

Doorless is that house,
And dark it is within ;
There thou art fast detained
And Death hath the key.
Loathsome is that earth-house.
And grim within to dwell.
There thou shalt dwell,
And worms shall divide thee.

Thus thou art laid,
And leavest thy friends ;
Thou hast no friend,
Who will come to thee,
Who will ever see
How that house pleaseth thee ;
Who will ever open
The door for thee
And descend after thee,
For soon thou art loathsome
And hateful to see.

KING CHRISTIAN.

A NATIONAL SONG OF DENMARK.

FROM THE DANISH OF JOHANNES EVALD.

KING CHRISTIAN stood by the lofty mast
 In mist and smoke ;
His sword was hammering so fast,
Through Gothic helm and brain it passed ;
Then sank each hostile hulk and mast,
 In mist and smoke.
" Fly ! " shouted they, " fly, he who can !
Who braves of Denmark's Christian
 The stroke ? "

Nils Juel gave heed to the tempest's roar,
 Now is the hour !
He hoisted his blood-red flag once more,
And smote upon the foe full sore,
And shouted loud, through the tempest's
  roar

"Now is the hour!"
"Fly!" shouted they, "for shelter **fly!**"
Of Denmark's Juel who can defy
    The power?"

North Sea! a glimpse of Wessel rent
    Thy murky sky!
Then champions to thine arms were sent;
Terror and Death glared where he went;
From the waves was heard a wail, that **rent**
    Thy murky sky!
From Denmark, thunders Tordenskiol',
Let each to Heaven commend his soul,
    And fly!

Path of the Dane to fame and might!
    Dark-rolling wave!
Receive thy friend, who, scorning **flight**
Goes to meet danger with despite,
Proudly as thou the tempest's might,
    Dark-rolling wave!
And amid pleasures and alarms,
And war and victory, be thine arms
    My grave!*

* Nils Juel was a celebrated Danish Admiral, **and**
Peder Wessel, a Vice-Admiral, who for his great prow-
ess received the popular title of Tordenskiold, or *Thun-
ders-shield*. In childhood he was a tailor's apprentice,
and rose to his high rank before the age of twenty-
eight, when he was killed in a duel.

THE HAPPIEST LAND.

FRAGMENT OF A MODERN BALLAD.

FROM THE GERMAN.

THERE sat one day in quiet,
 By an alehouse on the Rhine.
Four hale and hearty fellows,
 And drank the precious wine.

The landlord's daughter filled their cups,
 Around the rustic board ;
Then sat they all so calm and still,
 And spake not one rude word.

But, when the maid departed,
 A Swabian raised his hand,
And cried, all hot and flushed with wine,
 "Long live the Swabian land !

"The greatest kingdom upon earth
 Cannot with that compare ;
With all the stout and hardy men
 And the nut-brown maidens there."

"Ha!" cried a Saxon, laughing,—
   And dashed his beard with wine ;
"I had rather live in Lapland,
   Than that Swabian land of thine !

"The goodliest land on all the earth,
   It is the Saxon land !
There have I as many maidens
   As fingers on this hand ! "

"Hold your tongues! both Swabian and
       Saxon ! "
   A bold Bohemian cries ;
"If there's a heaven upon this earth,
   In Bohemia it lies.

"There the tailor blows the flute,
   And the cobbler blows the horn,
And the miner blows the bugle,
   Over mountain gorge and bourn."

      *   *   *   *

And then the landlord's daughter
   Up to heaven raised her hand,
And said, "Ye may no more contend,—
   There lies the happiest land ! "

THE WAVE.

FROM THE GERMAN OF TIEDGE.

"Whither, thou turbid wave?
Whither, with so much haste,
As if a thief wert thou?"

"I am the Wave of Life,
Stained with my margin's dust;
From the struggle and the strife
Of the narrow stream I fly
To the Sea's immensity,
To wash from me the slime
Of the muddy banks of Time."

THE DEAD.

FROM THE GERMAN OF KLOPSTOCK.

How they so softly rest,
All, all the holy dead,
Unto whose dwelling-place
Now doth my soul draw near!
How they so softly rest,
All in their silent graves,
Deep to corruption
Slowly down-sinking!

    And they no longer weep,
Here, where complaint is still!
And they no longer feel,
Here, where all gladness flies!
And, by the cypresses
Softly o'ershadowed,
Until the Angel
Calls them, they slumber!

THE BIRD AND THE SHIP.

FROM THE GERMAN OF MULLER.

"The rivers rush into the sea,
  By castle and town they go ;
The winds behind them merrily
  Their noisy trumpets blow.

"The clouds are passing far and high,
  We little birds in them play ;
And everything, that can sing and fly,
  Goes with us, and far away.

"I greet thee, bonny boat ! Whither, or
      whence
  With thy fluttering golden band ? "—
"I greet, thee, little bird ! To the wide sea
  I haste from the narrow land.

"Full and swollen is every sail ;
  I see no longer a hill,
I have trusted all to the sounding gale,
  And it will not let me stand still.

8   113

"And wilt thou, little bird, go with us?
  Thou mayest stand on the mainmast **tall,**
For full to sinking is my house
  With merry companions all."—

"I need not and seek not company,
  Bonny boat, I can sing all alone;
For the mainmast tall too heavy am I,
  Bonny boat, I have wings of my own.

"High over the sails, high over the mast,
  Who shall gainsay these joys?
When thy merry companions are still, **at**
      last,
  Thou shalt hear the sound of my voice.

"Who neither may rest, nor listen may,
  God bless them every one!
I dart away, in the bright blue day,
  And the golden fields of the sun.

"Thus do I sing my weary song,
  Wherever the four winds blow;
And this same song, my whole life **long,**
  Neither Poet nor Printer may know."

WHITHER?

FROM THE GERMAN OF MULLER.

I HEARD a brooklet gushing
  From its rocky fountain near,
Down into the valley rushing,
  So fresh and wondr   clear.

I know not what came o'er me,
  Nor who the counsel gave;
But I must hasten downward,
  All with my pilgrim-stave;

Downward, and ever farther,
  And ever the brook beside;
And ever fresher murmured,
  And ever clearer, the tide.

Is this the way I was going?
  Whither, O brooklet, say!
Thou hast, with thy soft murmur.
  Murmured my senses away

What do I say of a murmur?
  That can no murmur be ;
'T is the water-nymphs, that are singing
  Their roundelays under me.

Let them sing, my friend, let them murmur
  And wander merrily near ;
The wheels of a mill are going
  In every brooklet clear.

BEWARE!

FROM THE GERMAN.

I KNOW a maiden fair to see,
    Take care!
She can both false and friendly be,
    Beware! Beware!
    Trust her not,
She is fooling thee!

She has two eyes, so soft and brown,
    Take care!
She gives a side-glance and looks down,
    Beware! Beware!
    Trust her not,
She is fooling thee!

And she has hair of a golden hue,
    Take care!
And what she says, it is not true,
    Beware! Beware!
    Trust her not,
She is fooling thee!

She has a bosom as white as snow,
    Take care!
She knows how much it is best to show,
    Beware! Beware!
    Trust her not,
She is fooling thee!

She gives thee a garland woven fair.
    Take care!
It is a fool's-cap for thee to wear,
    Beware! Beware!
    Trust her not,
She is fooling thee!

SONG OF THE BELL.

FROM THE GERMAN.

Bell! thou soundest merrily,
When the bridal party
    To the church doth hie!
Bell! thou soundest solemnly,
When, on Sabbath morning,
    Fields deserted lie!

Bell! thou soundest merrily;
Tellest thou at evening
    Bed-time draweth nigh!
Bell! thou soundest mournfully;
Tellest thou the bitter
    Parting hath gone by!

Say! how canst thou mourn?
How canst thou rejoice?
    Thou art but metal dull!
And yet all our sorrowings,
And all our rejoicings,
    Thou dost feel them all!

God hath wonders many,
Which he cannot fathom !
    Placed within thy form !
When the heart is sinking,
Thou alone canst raise it,
    Trembling in the storm !

THE CASTLE BY THE SEA.

FROM THE GERMAN OF UHLAND.

"Hast thou seen that lordly castle,
   That Castle by the Sea?
Golden and red above it
   The clouds float gorgeously.

"And fain it would stoop downward,
   To the mirrored wave below;
And fain it would soar upward
   In the evening's crimson glow."

"Well have I seen that castle,
   That castle by the Sea,
And the moon above it standing,
   And the mist rise solemnly."

"The winds and the waves of ocean,
   Had they a merry chime?
Didst thou hear, from those lofty chambers
   The harp and the ministrel's rhyme?"

"The winds and the waves of ocean,
   They rested quietly,
But I heard on the gale a sound of wail,
   And tears came to mine eye."

"And sawest thou on the turrets
   The King and his royal bride?
And the wave of their crimson mantles?
   And the golden crown of pride?

"Led they not forth, in rapture,
   A beauteous maiden there?
Resplendent as the morning sun,
   Beaming with golden hair?"

"Well saw I the ancient parents,
   Without the crown of pride;
They were moving slow, in weeds of woe,
   No maiden was by their side!"

   III

THE BLACK KNIGHT.

FROM THE GERMAN OF UHLAND.

'T was Pentecost, the Feast of Gladness,
When woods and fields put off all sadness,
   Thus began the King and spake :
" So from the halls
Of ancient Hofburg's walls,
   A luxuriant Spring shall break.

Drums and trumpets echo loudly,
Wave the crimson banners proudly.
   From balcony the King looked on ;
In the play of spears,
Fell all the cavaliers,
   Before the monarch's stalwart son.

To the barrier of the fight
Rode at last a sable Knight,
   "Sir Knight! your name and scutcheon,
      say !".
   "Should I speak it here,
Ye would stand aghast with fear ;
   I'm a Prince of mighty sway !"

123

When he rode into the lists,
The arch of Heaven grew black with mists
   And the castle 'gan to rock.
At the first blow,
Fell the youth from saddle-bow,
   Hardly rises from the shock.

Pipe and viol call the dances,
Torch-light through the high halls glances;
   Waves a mighty shadow in;
With manner bland
Doth ask the maiden's hand,
   Doth with her the dance begin;

Danced in sable iron sark,
Danced a measure weird and dark,
   Coldly clasped her limbs around.
From breast and hair
Down fall from her the fair
   Flowerets, faded, to the ground.

To the sumptuous banquet came
Every Knight and every Dame.
   'Twixt son and daughter all distraught,
With mournful mind
The ancient King reclined,
   Gazed at them in silent thought.

Pale the children both did look,
But the guest a breaker took ;
   "Golden wine will make you whole !"
The children drank,
Gave many a courteous thank ;
   "O that draught was very cool !"

Each the father's breast embraces,
Son and daughter ; and their faces
   Colorless grow utterly.
Whichever way
Looks the fear-struck father gray,
   He beholds his children die.

"Woe ! the blessed children both
Takest thou in the joy of youth ;
   Take me, too, the joyless father !"
Spake the grim Guest,
From his hollow, cavernous breast ;
   "Roses in the spring I gather !"

SONG OF THE SILENT LAND.

FROM THE GERMAN OF SALIS.

Into the Silent Land!
Ah! who shall lead us thither?
Clouds in the evening sky more darkly
    gather,
And shattered wrecks lie thicker on the
    strand.
Who leads us with a gentle hand
Thither, O thither,
Into the Silent Land?

Into the Silent Land!
To you, ye boundless regions
Of all perfection! Tender morning-visions
Of beauteous souls! The Future's pledge
    and band!
Who in Life's battle firm doth stand,
Shall bear Hope's tender blossoms
Into the Silent Land!

O Land! O Land!
For all the broken-hearted
The mildest herald by our fate allotted,
Beckons, and with inverted torch doth **stand**
To lead us with a gentle hand
Into the land of the great **Departed,**
Into the Silent Land!

L'ENVOI.

Ye voices, that arose
After the Evening's close,
And whispered to my restless heart repose!

Go, breathe it in the ear
Of all who doubt and fear,
And say to them, " Be of good cheer!"

———

Ye sounds. so low and calm,
That in the groves of balm
Seemed to me like an angel's psalm!

Go, mingle yet once more
With the perpetual roar
Of the pine forest, dark and hoar!

———

Tongues of the dead, not lost,
But speaking from death's frost,
Like fiery tongues at Pentecost!

Glimmer, as funeral lamps,
Amid the chills and damps
Of the vast plain where Death encamps!

BALLADS

AND OTHER POEMS.

PREFACE.

THERE is one poem in this volume, in reference to which a few introductory remarks may be useful. It is *The Children of the Lord's Supper*, from the Swedish of Bishop Tegnér ; a poem which enjoys no inconsiderable reputation in the North of Europe, and for its beauty and simplicity merits the attention of English readers. It is an Idyl, descriptive of scenes in a Swedish village ; and belongs to the same class of poems as the *Luise* of Voss and the *Hermann und Dorothea* of Goethe. But the Swedish Poet has been guided by a surer taste than his German predecessors. His tone is pure and elevated ; and he rarely, if ever, mistakes what is trivial for what is simple.

There is something patriarchal still lingering about rural life in Sweden, which renders it a fit theme for song. Almost primeval simplicity reigns over that Northern land,— almost primeval solitude and stillness. You pass out from the gate of the city, and, as if by magic, the scene changes to a wild, woodland landscape. Around you are forests of fir. Overhead hang the long, fan-like branches, trailing with moss, and heavy with red and blue cones. Under foot is a carpet of yellow leaves; and the air is warm and balmy. On a wooden bridge you cross a little silver stream; and anon come forth into a pleasant and sunny land of farms. Wooden fences divide the adjoining fields. Across the road are gates, which are opened by troops of children. The peasants take off their hats as you pass; you sneeze, and they cry, "God bless you." The houses in the villages and smaller towns are all built of hewn timber, and for the most part painted red. The floors of the taverns are strewn with the fragrant tips of tir boughs. In many villages there are no taverns, and the peasants take turns in re-ceiving travelers. The thrifty housewife shows you into the best chamber, the walls of which are hung round with rude pictures from the Bible; and brings you her heavy silver spoons,—an heirloom,—to dip the curdled milk from the pan. You have oaten cakes baked some months before ; or bread with anise-seed and coriander in it, or perhaps a little pine bark.

Meanwhile the sturdy husband has brought his horses from the plough, and harnessed them to your carriage. Solitary travelers come and go in uncouth one-horse chaises. Most of them have pipes in their mouths, and hanging around their necks in front, a leather wallet, in which they carry tobacco, and the great bank-notes of the country, as large as your two hands. You meet, also, groups of Dalekarlian peasant women, traveling homeward or townward in pursuit of work. They walk barefoot, carrying in their hands their shoes, which have high heels under the hollow of the foot, and soles of birch bark.

Frequent, too, are the village churches, standing by the road-side, each in its own little garden of Gethsemane. In the parish register great events are doubtless recorded. Some old king was christened or buried in that church ; and a little sexton, with a rusty key, shows you the baptismal font, or the coffin. In the churchyard are a few flowers, and much green grass; and daily the shadow of the church spire, with its long tapering fingers counts the tombs, representing a dial-plate of human life, on which the hours and minutes are the graves of men. The stones are flat, and large, and low, and perhaps sunken, like the roofs of old houses. On some are armorial bearings ; on others only the initials of the poor tenants, with a date, as on the roofs of Dutch cottages. They all sleep with their heads to the westward. Each held a lighted taper in his hand when he died ; and in his coffin were placed his little heart-treasures, and a piece of money for his last journey. Babes that came lifeless into the world were carried in the arms of gray-haired old men to the only cradle they ever slept in ; and in the shroud of the dead mother were laid the little garments of the child that lived and died in her bosom. And over this scene the village pastor looks from his window in the stillness of midnight, and says in his heart, " How quietly they rest, all the departed ! "

Near the churchyard gate stands a poor-box, fastened to a post by iron bands, and secured by a padlock, with a sloping wooden roof to keep off the rain. If it be Sunday, the peasants sit on the church steps and con their psalm-books. Others are coming down the road with their beloved pastor, who talks to them of holy things from beneath his broad-brimmed hat. He speaks of fields and harvests, and of the parable of the sower, that went forth to sow. He leads them to the Good Shepherd, and to the pleasant pastures of the spirit-land. He is their patriarch, and, like Melchizedek, both priest and king, though he has no other throne than the church pulpit. The women carry psalm-books in their hands, wrapped in silk handkerchiefs, and listen devoutly to the good man's words. But the young men, like Gallio, care for none of these things. They are busy counting the plaits in the kirtles of the peasant girls, their number being an indication of the wearer's wealth. It may end in a wedding.

I will endeavor to describe a village wedding in Sweden. It shall be in summer time, that there may be flowers, and in a southern province, that the bride may be fair. The early song of the lark and of chanticleer are mingling in the clear morn-

ing air, and the sun, the heavenly bride-
groom with golden locks, arises in the east,
just as our earthly bridegroom with yellow
hair arises in the south. In the yard,
there is a sound of voices and trampling of
hoofs, and horses are led forth and saddled.
The steed that is to bear the bridegroom
has a bunch of flowers upon his forehead,
and a garland of corn-flowers around his
neck. Friends from the neighboring farms
come riding in, their blue cloaks streaming
to the wind; and finally the happy bride-
groom, with a whip in his hand, and a
monstrous nosegay in the breast of his
black jacket, comes forth from his chamber;
and then to horse and away, toward the
village where the bride already sits and
waits.

Foremost rides the Spokesman, followed
by some half-dozen village musicians. Next
comes the bridegroom between his two
groomsmen, and then forty or fifty friends
and wedding guests, half of them perhaps
with pistols and guns in their hands. A
kind of baggage-wagon brings up the rear,
laden with food and drink for these merry
pilgrims. At the entrance of every village

stands a triumphal arch, adorned with flowers and ribbons and evergreens; and as they pass beneath it the wedding guests fire a salute, and the whole procession stops. And straight from every pocket flies a black-jack, filled with punch or brandy. It is passed from hand to hand among the crowd; provisions are brought from the wagon, and after eating and drinking and hurrahing, the procession moves forward again, and at length draws near the house of the bride. Four heralds ride forward to announce that a knight and his attendants are in the neighboring forest, and pray for hospitality. " How many are you?" asks the bride's father. "At least three hundred," is the answer; and to this the host replies, "Yes; were you seven times as many, you should all be welcome; and in token thereof receive this cup." Whereupon each herald receives a can of ale; and soon after the whole jovial company comes storming into the farmer's yard, and, riding round the May-pole, which stands in the centre, alights amid a grand salute and flourish of music.

In the hall sits the bride, with a crown

upon her head and a tear in her eye, like
the Virgin Mary in old church paintings.
She is dressed in a red bodice and kirtle,
with loose linen sleeves. There is a gilded
belt around her waist; and around her
neck strings of golden beads, and a golden
chain. On the crown rests a wreath of
wild roses, and below it another of cypress.
Loose over her shoulders falls her flaxen
hair; and her blue innocent eyes are fixed
upon the ground. O thou good soul! thou
hast hard hands, but a soft heart! Thou
art poor. The very ornaments thou wearest
are not thine. They have been hired for
this great day. Yet art thou rich; rich
in health, rich in hope, rich in thy
first, young, fervent love. The blessing
of heaven be upon thee! So thinks the
parish priest, as he joins together the hands
of bride and bridegroom, saying in deep,
solemn tones, — "I give thee in marriage
this damsel, to be thy wedded wife in all
honor, and to share the half of thy bed, thy
lock and key, and every third penny which
you two may possess, or may inherit, and
all the rights which Upland's laws provide,
and the holy king Erik gave."

The dinner is now served, and the bride
sits between the bridegroom and the priest.
The Spokesman delivers an oration after the
ancient custom of his fathers. He interlards
it well with quotations from the Bible ; and
invites the Saviour to be present at this
marriage feast, as he was at the marriage
feast in Cana of Galilee. The table is not
sparingly set forth. Each makes a long
arm, and the feast goes cheerily on.
Punch and brandy pass round between the
courses, and here and there a pipe is smoked,
while waiting for the next dish. They sit
long at table ; but, as all things must have
an end, so must a Swedish dinner. Then
the dance begins. It is led off by the bride
and the priest, who perform a solemn
minuet together. Not till after midnight
comes the Last Dance. The girls form a
ring around the bride, to keep her from the
hands of the married women, who endeavor
to break through the magic circle, and seize
their new sister. After long struggling they
succeed ; and the crown is taken from her
head and the jewels from her neck, and her
bodice is unlaced and her kirtle taken off ;
and like a vestal virgin clad all in white she

goes, but it is to her marriage chamber, not
to her grave ; and the wedding guests fol-
low her with lighted candles in their hands.
And this is a village bridal.

Nor must I forget the suddenly changing
seasons of the Northern clime. There is no
long and lingering spring, unfolding leaf
and blossom one by one ;—no long and
lingering autumn, pompous with many-
colored leaves and the glow of Indian sum-
mers. But winter and summer are wonder-
ful, and pass into each other. The quail
has hardly ceased piping in the corn, when
winter from the folds of trailing clouds sows
broadcast over the land snow, icicles, and
rattling hail. The days wane apace. Ere
long the sun hardly rises above the horizon
or does not rise at all. The moon and the
stars shine through the day ; only, at noon,
they are pale and wan, and in the southern
sky a red, fiery glow, as of sunset, burns
along the horizon, and then goes out. And
pleasantly under the silver moon, and under
the silent, solemn stars, ring the steel-shoes
of the skaters on the frozen sea, and voices,
and the sound of bells.

And now the Northern Lights begin to

burn, faintly at first, like sunbeams playing
in the waters of the blue sea. Then a soft
crimson glow tinges the heavens. There is
a blush on the cheek of night. The colors
come and go ; and change from crimson to
gold, from gold to crimson. The snow is
stained with rosy light. Twofold from the
zenith, east and west, flames a fiery sword ;
and a broad band passes athwart the heavens,
like a summer sunset. Soft purple clouds
come sailing over the sky, and through their
vapory folds the winking stars shine white
as silver. With such pomp as this is Merry
Christmas ushered in, though only a single
star heralded the first Christmas. And in
memory of that day the Swedish peasants
dance on straw ; and the peasant girls
throw straws at the timbered roof of the hall,
and for every one that sticks in a crack shall
a groomsman come to their wedding. Merry
Christmas, indeed ! For pious souls there
shall be church songs and sermons, but for
Swedish peasants, brandy and nut brown
ale in wooden bowls ; and the great Yule-
cake crowned wtih a cheese, and garlanded
with apples, and upholding a three-armed
candlestick over the Christmas feast. They

may tell tales, too, of Jons Lundsbracka, and Lunkenfus, and the great Riddar Finke of Pingsdaga.*

And now the glad, leafy midsummer, full of blossoms and the song of nightingales, is come! Saint John has taken the flowers and festival of heathen Balder; and in every village there is a May-pole fifty feet high, with wreaths and roses and ribbons streaming in the wind, and a noisy weathercock on top to tell the village whence the wind cometh and whither it goeth. The sun does not set till ten o'clock at night; and the children are at play in the streets an hour later. The windows and doors are all open, and you may sit and read till midnight without a candle. O how beautiful is the summer night, which is not night, but a sunless yet unclouded day, descending upon earth with dews, and shadows, and refreshing coolness! How beautiful the long, mild twilight, which like a silver clasp unites to-day with yesterday! How beautiful the silent hour, when Morning and Evening thus sit together, hand in hand, beneath

* Titles of Swedish popular tales.

the starless sky of midnight! From the church-tower in the public square the bell tolls the hour, with a soft, musical chime; and the watchman, whose watch-tower is the belfry, blows a blast in his horn, for each stroke of the hammer, and four times, to the four corners of the heavens, in a sonorous voice he chaunts,—

> "Ho! watchman, ho!
> Twelve is the clock!
> God keep our town
> From fire and brand
> And hostile hand!
> Twelve is the clock!"

From his swallow's nest in the belfry he can see the sun all night long; and farther north the priest stands at his door in the warm midnight, and lights his pipe with a common burning glass.

I trust that these remarks will not be deemed irrelevant to the poem, but will lead to a clearer understanding of it. The translation is literal, perhaps to a fault. In no instance have I done the author a wrong, by introducing into his work any supposed improvements or embellishments of my

own. I have preserved even the measure ;
that inexorable hexameter, in which, it must
be confessed, the motions of the English
Muse are not unlike those of a prisoner danc-
ing to the music of his chains; and perhaps,
as Dr. Johnson said of the dancing dog,
"the wonder is not that she should do it so
well, but that she should do it at all."

Esaias Tegner, the author of this poem,
was born in the parish of By in Warmland,
in the year 1782. In 1799 he entered the
University of Lund, as a student ; and in
1812 was appointed Professor of Greek in
that institution. In 1824 he became Bishop
of Wexio, which office he still holds. He
stands first among all the poets of Sweden,
living or dead. His principal work is
Frithiofs Saga ; one of the most remark-
able poems of the age. This modern Scald
has written his name in immortal runes.
He is the glory and boast of Sweden ; a
prophet, honored in his own country, and
adding one more to the list of great names,
that adorn her history.

THE SKELETON IN ARMOR.

[The following Ballad was suggested to me while riding on the seashore at Newport. A year or two previous a skeleton had been dug up at Fall River, clad in broken and corroded armor; and the idea occurred to me of connecting it with the Round Tower at Newport, generally known hitherto as the Old Wind-Mill, though now claimed by the Danes as a work of their early ancestors. Professor Rafn, in the *Mémoires de la Société Royale des Antiquaires du Nord*, for 1838-1839, says:

"There is no mistaking in this instance the style in which the more ancient stone edifices of the North were constructed, the style which belongs to the Roman or Ante-Gothic architecture, and which, especially, after the time of Charlemagne, diffused itself from Italy over the whole of the West and the North of Europe, where it continued to predominate until the close of the 12th century; that style, which some authors have, from one of its most striking characteristics, called the round arch style, the same which in England is denominated Saxon and sometimes Norman architecture.

"On the ancient structure in Newport there are no ornaments remaining, which might possible have served to guide us in assigning the probably date of its erection. That no vestige whatever is found of the pointed arch nor any approximation to it, is indicative of

10

an earlier rather than of a later period. From such char-
acteristics as remain, however, we can scarcely form any
other inference than one, in which I am persuaded that
all, who are familiar with Old-Northern architecture,
will concur, THAT THIS BUILDING WAS ERECTED AT A
PERIOD DECIDEDLY NOT LATER THAN THE 12TH CAN-
TURY. This remark applies, of course, to the original
building only, and not to the alterations that it subse-
quently received; for there are several such alterations
in the upper part of the building which cannot be mis-
taken, and which were most likely occasioned by its be-
ing adapted in modern times to various uses, for ex-
ample as the substructure of a wind-mill, and latterly as
a hay magazine. To the same times may be referred the
windows, the fireplace, and the apertures made above
the columns. That this building could not have been
erected for a wind-mill, is what an architect will easily
discern."

I will not enter into a discussion of the point. It is
sufficiently well established for the purpose of a ballad;
though doubtless many an honest citizen of Newport,
who has passed his days within sight of the Round
Tower, will be ready to exclaim with Sancho; "God
bless me! did I not warn you to have a care of what
you were doing, for that it was nothing but a wind-mill;
and nobody could mistake it, but one who had the like
in his head."]

"SPEAK! speak! thou fearful guest!
Who, with thy hollow breast
Still in rude armor drest,
Comest to daunt me!

Wrapt not in Eastern balms,
But with thy fleshless palms
Stretched, as if asking alms,
    Why dost thou haunt me?"

Then, from those cavernous eyes
Pale flashes seemed to rise,
As when the Northern skies
    Gleam in December;
And, like the water's flow
Under December's snow,
Came a dull voice of woe
    From the heart's chamber.

"I was a Viking old!
My deeds, though manifold,
No Skald in song has told,
    No Saga taught thee!
Take heed, that in thy verse
Thou dost the tale rehearse,
Else dread a dead man's curse!
    For this I sought thee.

"Far in the Northern Land,
By the wild Baltic's strand,
I, with my childish hand,
    Tamed the ger-falcon;

And, with my skates fast-bound,
Skimmed the half-frozen Sound,
That the poor whimpering hound
    Trembled to walk on.

"Oft to his frozen lair
Tracked I the grisly bear,
While from my path the hare
    Fled like a shadow ;
Oft through the forest dark
Followed the were-wolf's bark,
Until the soaring lark
    Sang from the meadow.

"But when I older grew,
Joining a corsair's crew,
O'er the dark sea I flew
    With the marauders.
Wild was the life we led ;
Many the souls that sped,
Many the hearts that bled,
    By our stern orders.

" Many a wassail-bout
Wore the long Winter out ;
Often our midnight shout
    Set the cocks crowing,

As we the Berserk's tale
Measured in cups of ale,
Draining the oaken pail,
    Filled to o'erflowing.

"Once as I told in glee
Tales of the stormy sea,
Soft eyes did gaze on me,
    Burning yet tender ;
And as the white stars shine
On the dark Norway pine,
On that dark heart of mine
Fell their soft splendor.

" I wooed the blue-eyed maid,
Yielding, yet half afraid,
And in the forest's shade
    Our vows were plighted.
Under its loosened vest
Fluttered her little breast,
Like birds within their nest
    By the hawk frighted

"Bright in her father's hall
Shields gleamed upon the wall,
Loud sang the minstrels all,
    Chaunting his glory ;

When of old Hildebrand
I asked his daughter's hand,
Mute did the minstrels stand
    To hear my story,

" While the brown ale he quaffed,
Loud then the champion laughed,
And as the wind-gusts waft
    The sea-foam brightly,
So the loud laugh of scorn,
Out of those lips unshorn,
From the deep drinking-horn
    Blew the foam lightly.

" She was a Prince's child,
I but a Viking wild,
And though she blushed and smiled,
    I was discarded !
Should not the dove so white
Follow the sea-mew's flight,
Why did they leave that night
    Her nest unguarded?

" Scarce had I put to sea,
Bearing the maid with me, —
Fairest of all was she
    Among the Norsemen ! —

When on the white sea-strand,
Waving his armed hand,
Saw we old Hildebrand,
   With twenty horsemen.

"Then launched they to the blast,
Bent like a reed each mast,
Yet we were gaining fast,
   When the wind failed us :
And with a sudden flaw
Came round the gusty Skaw,
So that our foe we saw
   Laugh as he hailed us.

"And as to catch the gale
Round veered the flapping sail,
Death ! was the helmsman's hail,
   Death without quarter !
Mid-ships with iron keel
Struck we her ribs of steel ;
Down her black hulk did reel
   Through the black water !

"As with his wings aslant,
Sails the fierce cormorant,
Seeking some rocky haunt,
   With his prey laden,

So toward the open main,
Beating to sea again,
Through the wild huricane,
    Bore I the maiden.

"Three weeks we westward bore,
And when the storm was o'er,
Cloud-like we saw the shore
    Stretching to lee-ward;
There for my lady's bower
Built I the lofty tower,
Which, to this very hour,
    Stands looking sea-ward.

"There lived we many years;
Time dried the maiden's tears;
She had forgot her fears,
    She was a mother;
Death closed her mild blue eyes,
Under that tower she lies;
Ne'er shall the sun arise
    On such another!

"Still grew my bosom then,
Still as a stagnant fen!
Hateful to me were men,
    The sunlight hateful!

In the vast forest here,
Clad in my warlike gear,
Fell I upon my spear,
    O, death was grateful!

"Thus, seamed with many scars,
Bursting these prison bars,
Up to its native stars
    My soul ascended!
There from the flowing bowl
Deep drinks the warrior's soul,
Skoal! to the Northland! *Skoal!*"*
    —Thus the tale ended.

---

*In Scandinavia this is the customary salutation when drinking a health. I have slightly changed the orthography of the word, in order to preserve the correct pronunciation.

THE WRECK OF THE HESPERUS

It was the schooner Hesperus,
  That sailed the wintry sea;
And the skipper had taken his little daughter,
  To bear him company.

Blue were her eyes as the fairy-flax,
  Her cheeks like the dawn of day,
And her bosom white as the hawthorn
      buds,
  That ope in the month of May.

The skipper he stood beside the helm,
  With his pipe in his mouth,
And watched how the veering flaw did
      blow
  The smoke now West, now South.

Then up and spake an old Sailor,
  Had sailed the Spanish Main,
"I pray thee, put into yonder port,
  For I fear a hurricane.
    154

"Last night, the moon had a golden ring,
  And to-night no moon we see!"
The skipper he blew a whiff from his pipe,
  And a scornful laugh laughed he.

Colder and louder blew the wind,
  A gale from the Northeast;
The snow fell hissing in the brine,
  And the billows frothed like yeast.

Down came the storm, and smote amain,
  The vessel in its strength;
She shuddered and paused, like a frighted
      steed,
  Then leaped her cable's length.

"Come hither! come hither! my little
      daughter,
  And do not tremble so;
For I can weather the roughest gale,
  That ever wind did blow."

He wrapped her warm in his seaman's
      coat
  Against the stinging blast;
He cut a rope from a broken spar,
  And bound her to the mast.

"O father ! I hear the church-bells ring,
  O say, what may it be?"
"'T is a fog-bell on a rock-bound coast!"
  And he steered for the open sea.

"O father ! I hear the sound of guns,
  O say, what may it be?"
"Some ship in distress, that cannot live
  In such an angry sea!"

"O father ! I see a gleaming light,
  O say, what may it be?"
But the father answered never a word,
  A frozen corpse was he.

Lashed to the helm, all stiff and stark,
  With his face to the skies,
The lantern gleamed through the gleaming
      snow
  On his fixed and glassy eyes.

Then the maiden clasped her hands and
      prayed
  That saved she might be ;
And she thought of Christ, who stilled **the**
      wave,
  On the Lake of Galilee.

And fast through the midnight dark and
    drear,
  Through the whistling sleet and snow,
Like a sheeted ghost, the vessel swept
  Towards the reef of Norman's Woe,

And ever the fitful gusts between
  A sound came from the land ;
It was the sound of the trampling surf,
  On the rocks and the hard sea-sand.

The breakers were right beneath her bows,
  She drifted a dreary wreck,
And a whooping billow swept the crew
  Like icicles from her deck.

She struck where the white and fleecy
    waves
  Looked soft as carded wool,
But the cruel rocks, they gored her side
  Like the horns of an angry bull.

Her rattling shrouds, all sheathed in ice,
  With the masts went by the board ;
Like a vessel of glass, she strove and **sank**
  Ho ! Ho ! the breakers roared !

At daybreak, on the bleak sea-beach,
  A fisherman stood aghast,
To see the form of a maiden fair,
  Lashed close to a drifting mast.

The salt sea was frozen on her breast,
  The salt tears in her eyes ;
And he saw her hair, like the brown sea
    weed
  On the billows fall and rise.

Such was the wreck of the Hesperus,
  In the midnight and the snow !
Christ save us all from a death like this,
  On the reef of Norman's Woe !

THE LUCK OF EDENHALL.

FROM THE GERMAN OF UHLAND.

[The tradition, upon which this ballad is founded, and the "shards of the Luck of Edenhall," still exist in England. The goblet is in the possession of Sir Christopher Musgrave, Bart., of Eden Hall, Cumberland; and is not so entirely shattered, as the ballad leaves it.]

OF Edenhall, the youthful Lord
Bids sound the festal trumpet's call:
He rises at the banquet board,
And cries, 'mid the drunken revelers all,
" Now bring me the Luck of Edenhall!"

The butler hears the words with pain,
The house's oldest seneschal,
Takes slow from its silken cloth again
The drinking glass of crystal tall;
They call it the Luck of Edenhall.

Then said the Lord: "This glass to praise,
Fill with red wine from Portugal!"
The gray-beard with trembling hand obeys;

A purple light shines over all,
It beams from the Luck of Edenhall.

Then speaks the Lord, and waves it light,
"This glass of flashing crystal tall
Gave to my sires the Fountain-Sprite;
She wrote in it : *If this glass doth fall*
Farewell then, O Luck of Edenhall!

"'T was right a goblet the Fate should be
Of the joyous race of Edenhall !
Deep draughts drink we right willingly;
And willingly ring, with merry call,
Kling ! klang ! to the Luck of Edenhall ! "

First rings it deep, and full, and mild,
Like to the song of a nightingale ;
Then like the roar of a torrent wild ;
Then mutters at last like the thunder's
        fall,
The glorious Luck of Edenhall.

" For its keeper takes a race of might,
The fragile goblet of crystal tall ;
It has lasted longer than is right ;
Kling ! klang !—with a harder blow than all
Will I try the Luck of Edenhall ! "

As the goblet ringing flies apart,
Suddenly cracks the vaulted hall;
And through the rift, the wild flames start;
The guests in dust are scattered all.
With the breaking Luck of Edenhall!

In storms the foe, with fire and sword;
He in the night had scaled the wall,
Slain by the sword lies the youthful Lord,
But holds in his hand the crystal tall,
The shattered Luck of Edenhall.

On the morrow the butler gropes alone,
The gray-beard in the desert hall,
He seeks his Lord's burnt skeleton
He seeks in the dismal ruin's fall
The shards of the Luck of Edenhall.

"The stone wall," saith he, "doth fall
     aside,
Down must the stately columns fall;
Glass is this earth's Luck and Pride;
In atoms shall fall this earthly ball
One day like the Luck of Edenhall!"

11

THE ELECTED KNIGHT.

FROM THE DANISH.

[The following strange and somewhat mystical bal-
lad is from Nyerup and Rahbek's *Danske Viser* of the
Middle Ages. It seems to refer to the first preaching
of Christianity in the North, and to the institution of
Knight-Errantry. The three maidens I suppose to be
Faith, Hope, and Charity. The irregularities of the
original have been carefully preserved in the transla-
tion.]

Sir Oluf he rideth over the plain,
   Full seven miles broad and seven miles
      wide,
But never, ah never can meet with the man
   A tilt with him dare ride.

He saw under the hill-side
   A Knight full well equipped;
His steed was black, his helm was barred:
   He was riding at full speed.

He wore upon his spurs
   Twelve little golden birds;
162

Anon he spurred his steed with a clang,
  And there sat all the birds and sang.

He wore upon his mail
  Twelve little golden wheels ;
Anon in eddies the wild wind blew,
  And round and round the wheels they
      flew.

He wore before his breast
  A lance that was poised in rest ;
And it was sharper than diamond-stone,
  It made Sir Oluf's heart to groan.

He wore upon his helm
  A wreath of ruddy gold ;
And that gave him the Maidens Three,
  The youngest was fair to behold

Sir Oluf questioned the Knight eftsoon
  If he were come from heaven down ;
"Art thou Christ of Heaven," quoth he,
  "So will I yield me unto thee."

" I am not Christ the Great,
  Thou shalt not yield thee yet ;
I am an Unknown Knight,
  Three modest Maidens have me bedight."

"Art thou a Knight elected,
    And have three Maidens thee bedight
So shalt thou ride a tilt this day,
    For all the Maidens' honor!"

The first tilt they together rode,
    They put their steeds to the test;
The second tilt they together rode,
    They proved their manhood best.

The third tilt they together rode,
    Neither of them would yield;
The fourth tilt they together rode
    They both fell on the field.

Now lie the lords upon the plain,
    And their blood runs unto death;
Now sit the Maidens in the high tower,
    The youngest sorrows till death.

THE CHILDREN OF THE LORD'S SUPPER.

FROM THE SWEDISH OF BISHOP TEGNOR.

PENTECOST, day of rejoicing, had come. The
    church of the village
Stood gleaming white in the morning's sheen.
    On the spire of the belfry,
Tipped with a vane of metal, the friendly
    flames of the Spring-sun
Glanced like the tongues of fire, beheld by
    Apostles aforetime.
Clear was the heaven and blue, and May,
    with her cap crowned with roses,
Stood in her holiday dress in the fields, and
    the wind and the brooklet
Murmured gladness and peace, God's-peace!
    With lips rosy-tinted
Whispered the race of the flowers, and merry
    on balancing branches
Birds were singing their carol, a jubilant
    hymn to the Highest.

Swept and clean was the churchyard.
  Adorned like a leaf-woven arbor
Stood its old-fashioned gate; and within
  upon each cross of iron
Hung was a sweet-scented garland, new
  twined by the hands of affection.
Even the dial, that stood on a fountain
  among the departed
(There full a hundred years had it stood),
  was embellished with blossoms.
Like to the patriarch hoary, the sage of his
  kith and the hamlet,
Who on his birthday is crowned by chil-
  dren and children's children,
So stood the ancient prophet, and mute with
  pencil of iron
Marked on the table of stone, and measured
  the swift-changing moment,
While all around at his feet, an eternity
  slumbered in quiet.
Also the church within was adorned, for this
  was the season
In which the young, their parent's hope,
  and the loved-ones of heaven,
Should at the foot of the altar renew the
  vows of their baptism.

Therefore each nook and corner was swept
    and cleaned, and the dust was
Blown from the walls and ceiling, and from
    the oil-painted benches.
There stood the church like a garden ; the
    Feast of the Leafy Pavilions *
Saw we in living presentment. From noble
    arms on the church wall
Grew forth a cluster of leaves, and the
    preacher's pulpit of oak-wood
Budded once more anew, as aforetime the
    rod before Aaron.
Wreathed thereon was the Bible with leaves,
    and the dove, washed with silver,
Under its canopy fastened, a necklace had
    on of wind-flowers.
But in front of the choir, round the altar-
    piece painted by Horberg, †
Crept a garland gigantic ; and bright-curling
    tresses of angels
Peeped, like the sun from a cloud, out of the
    shadowy leaf-work.

* The Feast of the Tabernacles; in Swedish *Löi kyddohögtiden*, the Leaf-huts'-high-tide.

† The peasant-painter of Sweden. He is known chiefly by his altar-pieces in the village churches.

Likewise the lustre of brass, new-polished,
  blinked from the ceiling,
And for lights there were lilies of Pentecost
  set in the sockets.
Loud rang the bells already; the thronging
  crowd was assembled
Far from valleys and hills, to list to the holy
  preaching.
Hark! then roll forth at once the mighty
  tones from the organ,
Hover like voices from God, aloft like invis-
  ible spirits.
Like as Elias in heaven, when he cast off
  from him his mantle,
Even so cast off the soul its garments of
  earth; and with one voice
Chimed in the congregation, and sang an
  anthem immortal
Of the sublime Wallin,* of David's harp in
  the North-land
Tuned to the choral of Luther; the song on
  its powerful pinions
Took every living soul, and lifted it gently
  to heaven,

---

* A distinguished pulpit-orator and poet. He is par-
ticularly remarkable for the beauty and sublimity of his
psalms.

Ana every face did shine like the Holy One's
    face upon Tabor.

Lo! there entered then into the church the
    Reverend Teacher.

Father he hight and he was in the parish; a
    christianly plainness

Clothed from his head to his feet the old man
    of seventy winters.

Friendly was he to behold, and glad as the
    heralding angel

Walked he among the crowds, but still a
    contemplative grandeur

Lay on his forehead as clear, as on a moss-
    covered grave-stone a sunbeam.

As in his inspiration (an evening twilight
    that faintly

Gleams in the human soul, even now, from
    the day of creation)

Th' Artist, the friend of heaven, imagines
    Saint John when in Patmos ;—

Gray, with his eyes uplifted to heaven, so
    seemed then the old man ;

Such was the glance of his eye, and such
    were his tresses of silver.

All the congregation arose in the pews that
    were numbered.

But with a cordial look, to the right and the
    left hand, the old man

Nodding all hail and peace, disappeared in
    the innermost chancel.

Simply and solemnly now proceeded the
    Christian service,
Singing and prayer, and at last an ardent
    discourse from the old man.
Many a moving word and warning, that out
    of the heart came
Fell like the dew of the morning, like manna
    on those in the desert.
Afterwards, when all was finished, the
    Teacher reëntered the chancel,
Followed therein by the young. On the
    right hand the boys had their places
Delicate figures, with close-curling hair and
    cheeks rosy-blooming.
But on the left-hand of these, there stood the
    tremulous lilies,
Tinged with the blushing light of the morn-
    ing, the diffident maidens,—
Folding their hands in prayer, and their eyes
    cast down on the pavement.
Now came, with question and answer, the
    catechism. In the beginning
Answered the children with troubled and
    faltering voice, but the old man's

Glances of kindness encouraged them soon,
    and the doctrines eternal
Flowed, like the waters of fountains, so clear
    from lips unpolluted.
Whene'er the answer was closed, and as oft
    as they named the Redeemer,
Lowly louted the boys, and lowly the
    maidens all courtesied.
Friendly the Teacher stood, like an angel of
    light there among them,
And to the children explained he the holy,
    the highest, in few words,
Thorough, yet simple and clear, for sub-
    limity always is simple,
Both in sermon and song a child can seize
    on its meaning.
Even as the green-growing bud is unfolded
    when Spring-tide approaches
Leaf by leaf is developed, and, warmed by
    the radiant sunshine,
Blushes with purple and gold, till at last the
    perfected blossom
Opens its odorous chalice, and rocks with
    its crown in the breezes,
So was unfolded here the Christian lore of sal-
    vation,
Line by line from the soul of childhood.
    The fathers and mothers

Stood behind them in tears, and were glad
    at each well-worded answer.

Now went the old man up to the altar ;—
    and straightway transfigured
(So did it seem unto me) was then the affec-
    tionate Teacher.
Like the Lord's Prophet sublime, and awful
    as Death and as Judgment
Stood he, the God-commissioned, the soul-
    searcher, earthward descending,
Glances, sharp as a sword, into hearts, that
    to him were transparent
Shot he ; his voice was deep, was low like
    the thunder afar off.
So on a sudden transfigured he stood there
    he spake and he questioned.

"This is the faith of the Fathers, the faith
    the Apostles delivered,
This is moreover the faith whereunto I bap-
    tized you, while still ye
Lay on your mothers' breasts, and nearer
    the portals of heaven.
Slumbering received you then the Holy
    Church in its bosom ;

Wakened from sleep are ye now, and the
    light in its radiant splendor
Rains from the heaven downward ;—to-day
    on the threshold of childhood
Kindly she frees you again, to examine and
    make your election,
For she knows nought of compulsion, only
    conviction desireth.
This is the hour of your trial, the turning-
    point of existence,
Seed for the coming days ; without revocation
    departeth
Now from your lips the confession ; Bethink
    ye, before ye make answer !
Think not, O think not with guile to deceive
    the questioning Teacher.
Sharp is his eye to-day, and a curse ever
    rests upon falsehood.
Enter not with a lie on Life's journey ; the
    multitude hears you,
Brothers and sisters and parents, what dear
    upon earth is and holy
Standeth before your sight as a witness ; the
    Judge everlasting
Looks from the sun down upon you, and
    angels in waiting beside him
Grave your confession in letters of fire, upon
    tablets eternal.

Thus then,—believe ye in God, in the Father
    who this world created?

Him who redeemed it, the Son, and the
    Spirit where both are united?

Will ye promise me here (a holy promise!),
    to cherish

God more than all things earthly, and every
    man as a brother?

Will ye promise me here, to confirm your
    faith by your living,

Th' heavenly faith of affection! to hope, to
    forgive, and to suffer,

Be what it may your condition, and walk
    before God in uprightness?

Will ye promise me this before God and
    man?'—With a clear voice

Answered the young men Yes! and Yes!
    with lips softly-breathing

Answered the maidens eke. Then dissolved
    from the brow of the Teacher

Clouds with the thunders therein, and he
    spake on in accents more gentle,

Soft as the evening's breath, as harps by
    Babylon's rivers.

"Hail, then, hail to you all! To the
    heirdom of heaven be ye welcome!

Children no more from this day, but by cove-
    nant brothers and sisters !
Yet,—for what reason not children? Of
    such is the kingdom of heaven.
Here upon earth an assemblage of children,
    in heaven one father,
Ruling them as his own household,—forgiv-
    ing in turn and chastising,
That is of human life a picture, as Scripture
    has taught us.
Blessed are the pure before God! Upon
    purity and upon virtue
Resteth the Christian Faith ; she herself from
    on high is descended.
Strong as a man and pure as a child, is the
    sum of the doctrine,
Which the Godlike delivered, and on the
    cross suffered and died for.
O! as ye wander this day from childhood's
    sacred asylum
Downward and ever downward, and deeper
    in Age's chill valley,
O! how soon will ye come,—too soon !—
    and long to turn backward
Up to its hill-tops again, to the sun-illu-
    mined, where Judgment
Stood like a father before you, and Pardon,
    clad like a mother,

Gave you her hand to kiss, and the loving
     heart was forgiven,
Life was a play and your hands grasped
     after the roses of heaven !
Seventy years have I lived already; the
     Father eternal
Gave to me gladness and care ; but the love-
     liest hours of existence,
When I have steadfastly gazed in their eyes,
     I have instantly known them,
Known them all, all again ;—they were my
     childhood's acquaintance.
Therefore take from henceforth, as guides
     in the paths of existence,
Prayer, with her eyes raised to heaven, and
     Innocence, bride of man's childhood.
Innocence, child beloved, is a guest from
     the world of the blessed,
Beautiful, and in her hand a lily ; on life's
     roaring billows
Swings she in safety, she heeded them not,
     in the ship she was sleeping.
Calmly she gazes around in the turmoil of
     men ; in the desert
Angels descend and minister unto her ; she
     herself knoweth
Naught of her glorious attendance ; but fol-
     lows faithful and humble,

Follows so long as she may her friend ; O
    do not reject her,
For she cometh from God and she holdeth
    the keys of the heavens. —
Prayer is Innocence' friend ; and willingly
    flieth incessant
'Twixt the earth and the sky, the carrier-
    pigeon of heaven.
Son of Eternity, fettered in Time, and an
    exile, the Spirit
Tugs at his chains evermore, and struggles
    like flames ever upward.
Still he recalls with emotion his father's mani-
    fold mansions.
Thinks of the land of his fathers, where blos-
    somed more freshly the flowers,
Shone a more beautiful sun, and he played
    with the winged angels.
Then grows the earth too narrow, too close ;
    and homesick for heaven
Longs the wander r again ; and the Spirit's
    longings are worship ;
Worship is called his most beautiful hour,
    and its tongue is entreaty
Ah ! when the infinite burden of life de-
    scendeth upon us,
Crushes to earth our hope, and, under the
    earth, in the grave-yard, —

Then it is good to pray unto God; for his
    sorrowing children
Turns he ne'er from his door, but he heals
    and helps and consoles them.
Yet it is better to pray when all things are
    prosperous with us,
Pray in fortunate days, for life's most beauti-
    ful Fortune
Kneels down before the Eternal's throne;
    and, with hands interfolded,
Praises thankful and moved the only Giver
    of blessings.
Or do ye know, ye children, one blessing
    that comes not from Heaven?
What has mankind forsooth, the poor! that
    it has not received?
Therefore, fall in the dust and pray! The
    seraphs adoring
Cover with pinions six their face in the glory
    of him who
Hung his masonry pendant on naught, when
    the world he created.
Earth declareth his might, and the firmament
    uttereth his glory.
Races blossom and die, and stars fall down-
    ward from heaven,
Downward like withered leaves; at the last
    stroke of midnight, millenniums

Lay themselves down at his feet, and he sees
    them, but counts them as nothing.

Who shall stand in his presence? The wrath
    of the Judge is terrific,

Casting the insolent down at a glance. When
    he speaks in his anger

Hillocks skip like the kid, and the mountains
    leap like the roe-buck.

Yet,—why are ye afraid, ye children? This
    awful avenger,

Ah! is a merciful God! God's voice was
    not in the earthquake,

Not in the fire, nor the storm, but it was in
    the whispering breezes.

Love is the root of creation; God's essence;
    worlds without number

Lie in his bosom like children; he made
    them for this purpose only.

Only to love and to be loved again, he
    breathed forth his spirit

Into the slumbering dust, and upright stand-
    ing, it laid its

Hand on its heart, and felt it was warm with
    a flame out of heaven.

Quench, O quench not that flame! It is the
    breath of your being.

Love is life, but hatred is death. Not father,
    nor mother

Loved you, as God has loved you ; for it
    was that you may be happy
Gave he his only son. When he bowed
    down his head in the death-hour
Solemnized Love its triumph ; the sacrifice
    then was completed.
Lo ! then was rent on a sudden the vail of
    the temple, dividing
Earth and heaven apart, and the dead from
    their sepulchers rising
Whispered with pallid lips and low in the
    ears of each other
Th' answer, but dreamed of before, to crea-
    tion's enigma,—Atonement !
Depths of Love are Atonement's depths, for
    Love is Atonement.
Therefore, child of mortality, love thou the
    merciful Father ;
Wish what the Holy One wishes, and not
    from fear, but affection ;
Fear is the virtue of slaves ; but the heart
    that loveth is willing ;
Perfect was before God, and perfect is Love,
    and Love only.
Lovest thou God as thou oughtest, then
    lovest thou likewise thy brethren :

One is the sun in Heaven, and one, only one
    is Love also.

Bears not each human figure the godlike
    stamp on his forehead?

Readest thou not in his face thine origin?
    Is he not sailing

Lost like thyself on an ocean unknown, and
    is he not guided

By the same stars that guide thee? Why
    shouldst thou hate then thy brother?

Hateth he thee, forgive! For 't is sweet to
    stammer one letter

Of the Eternal's language;—on earth it is
    called Forgiveness!

Knowest thou Him, who forgave, with the
    crown of thorns round his temples?

Earnestly prayed for his foes, for his mur-
    derers? Say, dost thou know him?

Ah! thou confessest his name, so follow
    likewise his example,

Think of thy brother no ill, but throw a vail
    over his failings,

Guide the erring aright; for the good, the
    heavenly shepherd

Took the lost lamb in his arms, and bore it
    back to its mother.

This is the fruit of Love, and it is by its fruits
    that we know it.
Love is the creature's welfare, with God;
    but Love among mortals
Is but an endless sigh! He longs, and en-
    dures, and stands waiting,
Suffers and yet rejoices, and smiles with
    tears on his eyelids.
Hope,—so is called upon earth, his recom-
    pense.—Hope, the befriending,
Does what she can, for she points evermore
    up to heaven, and faithful
Plunges her anchor's peak in the depths of
    the grave, and beneath it
Paints a more beautiful world, a dim, but a
    sweet play of shadows!
Races, better than we, have leaned on her
    wavering promise,
Having naught else beside Hope. Then
    praise we our Father in Heaven,
Him, who has given us more; for to us has
    Hope been illumined,
Groping no longer in night; she is Faith,
    she is living assurance.
Faith is enlightened Hope; she is light, is
    the eye of affection,

Dreams of the longing interprets, and carves
    their visions in marble.

Faith is the sun of life ; and her countenance
    shines like the Prophet's,

For she has looked upon God ; the heaven
    on its stable foundation

Draws she with chains down to earth, and
    the New Jerusalem sinketh

Splendid with portals twelve in golden
    vapors descending.

There enraptured she wanders, and looks at
    the figures majestic,

Fears not the winged crowd, in the midst of
    them all is her homestead.

Therefore love and believe ; for works will
    follow spontaneous

Even as day does the sun ; the Right from
    the Good is an offspring,

Love in a bodily shape ; and Christian works
    are no more than

Animate Love and faith, as flowers are the
    animate spring-tide.

Works do follow us all unto God ; there
    stand and bear witness

Not what they seemed, —but what they were
    only. Blessed is he who

Hears their confession secure ; they are
　　mute upon earth until death's hand
Opens the mouth of the silent.　Ye children,
　　does Death e'er alarm you ?
Death is the brother of Love, twin-brother
　　is he, and is only
More austere to behold.　With a kiss upon
　　lips that are fading
Takes he the soul and departs, and rocked
　　in the arms of affection,
Places the ransomed child, new born, 'fore
　　the face of its father.
Sounds of his coming already I hear,—see
　　dimly his pinions,
Swart as the night, but with stars strewn
　　upon them !　I fear not before him.
Death is only release, and in mercy is mute.
　　On his bosom
Freer breathes, in its coolness, my breast ;
　　and face to face standing
Look I on God as he is, a sun unpolluted by
　　vapors ;
Look on the light of the ages I loved, the
　　spirits majestic,
Nobler, better than I ; they stand by the
　　throne all transfigured,

Vested in white, and with harps of gold, and
 are singing an anthem,
Writ in the climate of heaven, in the lan-
 guage spoken by angels.
You, in like manner, ye children beloved,
 he one day shall gather,
Never forgets he the weary ;—then welcome,
 ye loved ones, hereafter !
Meanwhile forget not the keeping of vows,
 forget not the promise,
Wander from holiness onward to holiness ;
 earth shall ye heed not ;
Earth is but dust and heaven is light ; I
 have pledged you to heaven.
God of the Universe, hear me ! thou fountain
 of Love everlasting,
Hark to the voice of thy servant ! I send
 up my prayer to thy heaven !
Let me hereafter not miss at thy throne one
 spirit of all these,
Whom thou hast given me here ! I have
 loved them all like a father.
May they bear witness for me, that I taught
 them the way of salvation,
Faithful, so far as I knew of thy word ; again
 may they know me,

Fall on their Teacher's breast, and before thy
        face may I place them,
Pure as they now are, but only more tried,
        and exclaiming with gladness,
Father, lo! I am here, and the children,
        whom thou hast given me!"

Weeping he spake in these words; and now
        at the beck of the old man
Knee against knee they knitted a wreath
        round the altar's enclosure.
Kneeling he read then the prayers of the con-
        secration, and softly
With him the children read; at the close,
        with tremulous accents,
Asked he the peace of heaven, a benediction
        upon them.
Now should have ended his task for the day;
        the following Sunday
Was for the young appointed to eat of the
        Lord's holy Supper.
Sudden, as struck from the clouds, stood the
        Teacher silent and laid his
Hand on his forehead, and cast his looks up-
        ward; while thoughts high and holy
Flew through the midst of his soul, and his
        eyes glanced with wonderful bright-
        ness.

"On the next Sunday, who knows ! perhaps
    I shall rest in the grave-yard !
Some one perhaps of yourselves, a lily
    broken untimely,
Bow down his head to the earth ; why delay
    I ? the hour is accomplished.
Warm is the heart ;—I will so ! for to-day
    grows the harvest of heaven.
What I began accomplish I now ; for what
    failing therein is
I, the old man, will answer to God and the
    reverend father
Say to me only, ye children, ye denizens
    new-come in heaven,
Are ye ready this day to eat of the bread of
    Atonement ?
What it denoteth, that know ye full well, I
    have told it you often.
Of the new covenant a symbol it is, of Atone-
    ment a token,
'Stablished between earth and heaven. Man
    by his sins and transgressions
Far has wandered from God, from his es-
    sence. 'Twas in the beginning
Fast by the Tree of Knowledge he fell, and
    it hangs its crown o'er the

Fall to this day ; in the Thought is the Fall ;
    in the Heart the Atonement.

Infinite is the Fall, the Atonement infinite
    likewise.

See! behind me, as far as the old man re-
    members, and forward,

Far as Hope in her flight can reach with her
    wearied pinions,

Sin and Atonement incessant go through the
    lifetime of mortals.

Brought forth is sin full-grown ; but Atone-
    ment sleeps in our bosoms

Still as the cradled babe ; and dreams of
    heaven and of angels

Cannot wake to sensation ; is like the tones
    in the harp's strings,

Spirits imprisoned, that wait evermore the
    deliverer's finger.

Therefore, ye children beloved, descended
    the Prince of Atonement,

Woke the slumberer from sleep, and he
    stands now with eyes all resplendent,

Bright as the vault of the sky, and battles
    with Sin and o'ercomes her.

Downward to earth he came and transfigured
    thence reascended,

Not from the heart in likewise, for there he
    still lives in the Spirit,
Loves and atones evermore. So long as
    Time is, is Atonement.
Therefore with reverence receive this day
    her visible token.
Tokens are dead if the things do not live.
    The light everlasting
Unto the blind man is not, but is born of the
    eye that has vision.
Neither in bread nor in wine, but in the
    heart that is hallowed
Lieth forgiveness enshrined ; the intention
    alone of amendment.
Fruits of the earth ennobles to heavenly
    things, and removes all
Sin and the guerdon of sin. Only Love with
    his arms wide extended,
Penitence weeping and praying ; the Will
    that is tried, and whose gold flows
Purified forth from the flames ; in a word,
    mankind by Atonement
Breaketh Atonement's bread, and drinketh
    Atonement's wine cup.
But he who cometh up hither, unworthy,
    with hate in his bosom,

Scoffing at men and at God, is guilty **of**
    Christ's blessed body,

And the Redeemer's blood !   To himself he
    eateth and drinketh

Death and doom!   And from this, preserve
    us, thou heavenly Father !

Are ye ready, ye children, to eat of the bread
    of Atonement ? "

Thus with emotion he asked, and together
    answered the children

Yes ! with deep sobs interrupted.   Then
    read he the due supplications,

Read the Form of Communion, and in
    chimed the organ and anthem ;

O ! Holy Lamb of God, who takest away
    our transgressions,

Hear us ! give us thy peace ! have mercy,
    have mercy upon us !

Th' old man, with trembling hand, and
    heavenly pearls on his eyelids,

Filled now the chalice and paten, and dealt
    round the mystical symbols.

O ! then seemed it to me, as if God, with the
    broad eye of mid-day,

Clearer looked in at the windows, and all
    the trees in the churchyard

Bowed down their summits of green, and the
      grass on the graves 'gan to shiver.
But in the children (I noted it well ; I knew
      it) there ran a
Tremor of holy rapture along through their
      icy-cold members.
Decked like an altar before them, there stood
      the green earth, and above it
Heaven opened itself, as of old before
      Stephen ; there saw they
Radiant in glory the Father, and on his right
      hand the Redeemer.
Under them hear they the clang of harp-
      strings, and angels from gold clouds
Beckon to them like brothers, and fan with
      their pinions of purple.

   Closed was the Teacher's task, and with
      heaven in their hearts and their faces,
Up rose the children all, and each bowed
      him, weeping full sorely,
Downward to kiss that reverend hand, but
      all of them pressed he
Moved to his bosom, and laid, with a prayer,
      his hands full of blessings,
Now on the holy breast, and now on the
      innocent tresses.

MISCELLANEOUS.

[The following poems, with one exception, were written at sea, in the latter part of October. I had not then heard of Dr. Channing's death. Since that event, the poem addressed to him is no longer appropriate. I have decided, however, to let it remain as it was written, a feeble testimony of my admiration for a great and good man.]

THE VILLAGE BLACKSMITH.

UNDER a spreading chestnut tree
   The village smithy stands ;
The smith, a mighty man is he,
   With large and sinewy hands ;
And the muscles of his brawny arms
   Are strong as iron bands.

His hair is crisp, and black, and long,
   His face is like the tan ;
His brow is wet with honest sweat,
   He earns whate'er he can,
And looks the whole world in the face,
   For he owes not any man.

Week in, week out, from morn till night,
   You can hear his bellows blow ;
You can hear him swing his heavy sledge,
   With measured beat and slow,
Like a sexton ringing the village bell,
   When the evening sun is low.

And children coming home from school
    Look in at the open door ;
They love to see the flaming forge,
    And hear the bellows roar,
And catch the burning sparks that fly
    Like chaff from a threshing floor.

He goes on Sunday to the church,
    And sits among his boys ;
He hears the parson pray and preach,
    He hears his daughter's voice,
Singing in the village choir,
    And it makes his heart rejoice.

It sounds to him like her mother's voice,
    Singing in Paradise !
He needs must think of her once more,
    How in the grave she lies ;
And with his hard, rough hand he wipes
    A tear out of his eyes.

Toiling,—rejoicing,—sorrowing,
    Onward through life he goes ;
Each morning sees some task begun,
    Each evening sees it close ;
Something attempted, something done
    Has earned a night's repose.

Thanks, thanks to thee, my worthy friend,
  For the lesson thou hast taught !
Thus at the flaming forge of life
  Our fortunes must be wrought ;
Thus on its sounding anvil shaped
  Each burning deed and thought !

ENDYMION.

THE rising moon has hid the stars ;
Her level rays, like golden bars,
    Lie on the landscape green,
    With shadows brown between.

And silver white the river gleams,
As if Diana, in her dreams,
    Had dropt her silver bow
    Upon the meadows low.

On such a tranquil night as this,
She woke Endymion with a kiss,
    When, sleeping in the grove,
    He dreamed not of her love.

Like Dian's kiss ; unasked, unsought,
Love gives itself, but is not bought ;
    Nor voice, nor sound betrays
    Its deep, impassioned gaze.

It comes,—the beautiful, the free,
The crown of all humanity,—
    In silence and alone
    To seek the elected one.

It lifts the boughs, whose shadows deep,
Are Life's oblivion, the soul's sleep,
    And kisses the closed eyes
    Of him, who slumbering lies.

O, weary hearts! O, slumbering eyes!
O, drooping souls, whose destinies
    Are fraught with fear and pain,
    Ye shall be loved again!

No one is so accursed by fate,
No one so utterly desolate,
    But some heart, though unknown,
    Responds unto his own.

Responds,—as if with unseen wings,
A breath from heaven had touched its strings;
    And whispers, in its song,
    "Where hast thou stayed so long?"

THE TWO LOCKS OF HAIR.

FROM THE GERMAN OF PFIZER.

A YOUTH, light-hearted and content,
   I wander through the world;
Here, Arab-like, is pitched my tent
   And straight again is furled.

Yet oft I dream, that once a wife
   Close in my heart was locked,
And in the sweet repose of life
   A blessed child I rocked.

I wake! Away that dream,—away!
   Too long did it remain!
So long, that both by night and day
   It ever comes again.

The end lies ever in my thought;
   To a grave so cold and deep
The mother beautiful was brought;
   Then dropt the child asleep.

But now the dream is wholly o'er,
  I bathe mine eyes and see ;
And wander through the world once more,
  A youth so light and free.

Two locks,—and they are wondrous fair,—
  Left me that vision mild ;
The brown is from the mother's hair,
  The blond is from the child.

And when I see that lock of gold,
  Pale grows the evening-red ;
And when the dark lock I behold,
  I wish that I were dead.

IT IS NOT ALWAYS MAY.

No hay pàjaros en los nidos de antaño.
Spanish Proverb.

THE sun is bright,—the air is clear ;
  The darting swallows soar and sing,
And from the stately elms I hear
  The blue-bird prophesying Spring.

So blue yon winding river flows,
  It seems an outlet from the sky,
Where waiting till the west wind blows,
  The freighted clouds at anchor lie.

All things are new ;—the buds, the leaves,
  That gild the elm-tree's nodding crest,
And even the nest beneath the eaves ;—
  There are no birds in last year's nest !

All things rejoice in youth and love,
  The fullness of their first delight !
And learn from the soft heavens above
  The melting tenderness of night.

Maiden, that read'st this simple rhyme,
  Enjoy thy youth, it will not stay ;
Enjoy the fragrance of thy prime,
  For O ! it is not always May !

Enjoy the Spring of Love and Youth,
  To some good angel leave the rest ;
For Time will teach thee soon the truth,
  There are no birds in last year's nest !

THE RAINY DAY.

THE day is cold, and dark, and dreary ;
It rains, and the wind is never weary ;
The vine still clings to the mouldering wall,
But at every gust the dead leaves fall,
    And the day is dark and dreary.

My life is cold, and dark, and dreary ;
It rains, and the wind is never weary ;
My thoughts still cling to the mouldering Past,
But the hopes of youth fall thick in the blast,
    And the days are dark and dreary.

Be still, sad heart ! and cease repining ;
Behind the clouds is the sun still shining ;
Thy fate is the common fate of all,
Into each life some rain must fall,
    Some days must be dark and dreary.

GOD'S-ACRE.

I **like** that ancient Saxon phrase, which calls
    The burial-ground God's-Acre! It is just;
It consecrates each grave within its walls,
    And breathes a benison o'er the sleeping
        dust.

God's-Acre! Yes, that blessed name im-
      parts
    Comfort to those, who in the grave have
      sown
The seed, that they had garnered in their
      hearts,
    Their bread of life, alas! no more their
      own.

Into its furrows shall we all be cast,
    In the sure faith, that we shall rise again
At the great harvest, when the archangel's
      blast
    Shall winnow, like a fan, the chaff and
      grain.

Then shall the good stand in immortal
    bloom,
  In the fair gardens of that second birth ;
And each bright blossom, mingle its per-
    fume
  With that of flowers, which never bloomed
    on earth.

With thy rude ploughshare, Death, turn up
    the sod,
  And spread the furrow for the seed we sow;
This is the field and Acre of our God.
  This is the place, where human harvests
    grow !

TO THE RIVER CHARLES.

River! that in silence windest
  Through the meadows, bright and free,
Till at length thy rest thou findest
  In the bosom of the sea!

Four long years of mingled feeling,
  Half in rest, and half in strife,
I have seen thy waters stealing
  Onward, like the stream of life.

Thou hast taught me, Silent River!
  Many a lesson, deep and long;
Thou hast been a generous giver;
  I can give thee but a song.

Oft in sadness and in illness,
  I have watched thy current glide,
Till the beauty of its stillness
  Overflowed me, like a tide.

And in better hours and brighter,
  When I saw thy waters gleam,

I have felt my heart beat lighter,
   And leap onward with thy stream.

Not for this alone I love thee,
   Nor because, thy waves of blue
From celestial seas above thee
   Take their own celestial hue.

Where yon shadowy woodlands hide thee,
   And thy waters disappear,
Friends I love have dwelt beside thee,
   And have made thy margin dear.

More than this ;—thy name reminds me
   Of three friends, all true and tried ;
And that name, like magic, binds me
   Closer, closer to thy side.

Friends my soul with joy remembers !
   How like quivering flames they start,
When I fan the living embers
   On the hearth-stone of my heart !

'Tis for this, thou Silent River !
   That my spirit leans to thee ;
Thou hast been a generous giver,
   Take this idle song from me.

BLIND BARTIMEUS.

Blind Bartimeus at the gates
Of Jericho in darkness waits ;
He hears the crowd ;—he hears a breath
Say, "It is Christ of Nazareth ! "
And calls, in tones of agony,
Ἰησοῦ, ἐλέησόν με !

The thronging multitudes increase ;
Blind Bartimeus, hold thy peace !
But still, above the noisy crowd,
The beggar's cry is shrill and loud ;
Until they say, "He calleth thee ! "
Θάρσει, ἔγειραι, φωνεῖ σε !

Then saith the Christ, as silent stands
The crowd, "What wilt thou at my hands ? "
And he replies, "O give me light !
Rabbi, restore the blind man's sight."
And Jesus answers, Ὕπαγε·
Ἡ πίστις σου σέσωκέ σε !

Ye that have eyes, yet cannot see,
In darkness and in misery,
Recall those mighty Voices Three,
Ἰησοῦ, ἐλέησόν με!
Θάρσει, ἔγειραι, ὕπαγε!
Ἡ πίστις σου σέσωκέ σέ!

THE GOBLET OF LIFE.

FILLED is Life's goblet to the brim;
And though my eyes with tears are dim
I see its sparkling bubbles swim,
And chant a melancholy hymn
    With solemn voice and slow.

No purple flowers,—no garlands green,
Conceal the goblet's shade or sheen,
Nor maddening draughts of Hippocrene,
Like gleams of sunshine, flash between
    Thick leaves of mistletoe.

This goblet, wrought with curious art,
Is filled with waters, that upstart,
When the deep fountains of the heart,
By strong convulsions rent apart,
    Are running all to waste.

And as it mantling passes round,
With fennel is it wreathed and crowned,

Whose seed and foliage sun-imbrowned
Are in its waters steeped and drowned,
    And give a bitter taste.

Above the lowly plants it towers,
The fennel, with its yellow flowers,
And in an earlier age than ours
Was gifted with the wondrous powers,
    Lost vision to restore.

It gave new strength, and fearless **mood ;**
And gladiators, fierce and rude,
Mingled it in their daily food ;
And he who battled and subdued,
    A wreath of fennel wore.

Then in Life's goblet freely press,
The leaves that give it bitterness,
Nor prize the colored waters less,
For in thy darkness and distress
    New light and strength they **give !**

And he who has not learned to know
How false its sparkling bubbles show,
How bitter are the drops of woe,
With which its brim may overflow,
    He has not learned to live.

The prayer of Ajax was for light;
Through all that dark and desperate fight,
The blackness of that noonday night,
He asked but the return of sight,
    Te see his foeman's face.

Let our unceasing, earnest prayer
Be, too, for light,—for strength to bear
Our portion of the weight of care,
That crushes into dumb despair
    One half the human race.

O suffering, sad humanity!
O ye afflicted ones, who lie
Steeped to the lips in misery,
Longing, and yet afraid to die,
    Patient, though sorely tried!

I pledge you in this cup of grief,
Where floats the fennel's bitter leaf!
The Battle of our Life is brief,
The alarm,—the struggle,—the relief,—
    Then sleep we side by side.

MAIDENHOOD.

Maiden ! with the meek, brown eyes,
In whose orbs a shadow lies
Like the dusk in evening skies !

Thou whose locks outshine the sun,
Golden tresses, wreathed in one,
As the braided streamlets run !

Standing, with reluctant feet,
Where the brook and river meet,
Womanhood and childhood fleet !

Gazing, with a timid glance,
On the brooklet's swift advance,
On the river's broad expanse !

Deep and still, that gliding stream
Beautiful to thee must seem,
As the river of a dream.

Then why pause with indecision,
When bright angels in thy vision
Beckon thee to fields Elysian ?

Seest thou shadows sailing by,
As the dove, with startled eye,
Seest the falcon's shadow fly?

Hearest thou voices on the shore,
That our ears perceive no more,
Deafened by the cataract's roar?

O, thou child of many prayers!
Life hath quicksands,—Life hath **snares!**
Care and age come unawares!

Like the swell of some sweet tune,
Morning rises into noon,
May glides onward into June.

Childhood is the bough, where slumbered
Birds and blossom many-numbered;—
Age, that bough with snows encumbered.

Gather, then, each flower that grows,
When the young heart overflows,
To embalm that tent of snow.

Bear a lily in thy hand;
Gates of brass cannot withstand
One touch of that magic wand.

Bear through sorrow, wrong, and ruth,
In thy heart the dew of youth,
On thy lips the smile of truth.

O, that dew, like balm, shall steal
Into wounds, that cannot heal,
Even as sleep our eyes doth seal;

And that smile, like sunshine, dart
Into many a sunless heart,
For a smile of God thou art.

EXCELSIOR.

THE shades of night were falling fast,
As through an Alpine village passed
A youth, who bore, 'mid snow and ice,
A banner with the strange device
　　　　Excelsior !

His brow was sad ; his eye beneath,
Flashed like a falchion from its sheath,
And like a silver clarion rung
The accents of that unknown tongue,
　　　　Excelsior !

In happy homes he saw the light
Of household fires gleam warm and **bright**;
Above, the spectral glaciers shone,
And from his lips escaped a groan,
　　　　Excelsior !

"Try not the Pass !" the old man **said** ;
"Dark lowers the tempest overhead,

The roaring torrent is deep and wide ! "
And loud that clarion voice replied
       Excelsior !

"O stay," the maiden said, "and rest
Thy weary head upon this breast ! "
A tear stood in his bright blue eye,
But still he answered, with a sigh,
       Excelsior !

"Beware the pine-tree's withered branch !
Beware the awful avalanche ! "
This was the peasant's last Good-night,
A voice replied, far up the height,
       Excelsior !

At break of day, as heavenward
The pious monks of Saint Bernard
Uttered the oft-repeated prayer,
A voice cried through the startled air
       Excelsior !

A traveler, by the faithful hound,
Half-buried in the snow was found,
Still grasping in his hand of ice
That banner with the strange device
       Excelsior !

There in the twilight cold and gray,
Lifeless, but beautiful, he lay,
And from the sky, serene and far,
A voice fell, like a falling star,
　　　Excelsior !

POEMS ON SLAVERY.

POEMS ON SLAVERY.

The noble horse,
That, in his fiery youth, from his wide nostrils
Neighed courage to his rider, and brake through
Groves of opposed pikes, bearing his lord
Safe to triumphant victory, old or wounded,
Was set at liberty and freed from service.
The Athenian mules, that from the quarry drew
Marble, hewed for the Temple of the Gods,
The great work ended, were dismissed and fed
At the public cost; nay, faithful dogs have found
Their sepulchres; but man, to man more cruel,
Appoints no end to the sufferings of his slave.

MASSINGER.

TO WILLIAM E. CHANNING.

THE pages of thy book I read,
    And as I closed each one,
My heart, responding, ever said,
    "Servant of God! well done!"

Well done! Thy words are great and bold;
    At times they seem to me,

Like Luther's, in the days of old,
   Half-battles for the free.

Go on, until this land revokes
   The old and chartered Lie,
The feudal curse, whose whips and yokes
   Insult humanity.

A voice is ever at thy side
   Speaking in tones of might,
Like the prophetic voice, that cried
   To John in Patmos, "Write!"

Write! and tell out this bloody tale,
   Record this dire eclipse,
This Day of Wrath, this Endless Wail,
   This dread Apocalypse!

THE SLAVE'S DREAM.

BESIDE the ungathered rice he lay,
　　His sickle in his hand;
His breast was bare, his matted hair
　　Was buried in the sand.
Again, in the mist and shadow of sleep,
　　He saw his Native Land.

Wide through the landscape of his dreams
　　The lordly Niger flowed;
Beneath the palm-trees on the plain
　　Once more a king he strode;
And heard the tinkling caravans
　　Descend the mountain-road.

He saw once more his dark-eyed queen
　　Among her children stand;
They clasped his neck, they kissed his cheeks,
　　They held him by the hand!—
A tear burst from the sleeper's lids
　　And fell into the sand.

And then at furious speed he rode
    Along the Niger's bank ;
His bridle-reins were golden chains,
    And, with a martial clank,
At each leap he could feel his scabbard of
        steel
    Smiting his stallion's flank.

Before him, like a blood-red flag,
    The bright flamingoes flew ;
From morn till night he followed their flight,
    O'er plains where the tamarind grew,
Till he saw the roofs of Caffre huts,
    And the ocean rose to view.

At night he heard the lion roar,
    And the hyæna scream,
And the river-horse, as he crushed the reeds
    Beside some hidden stream ;
And it passed, like a glorious roll of drums,
    Through the triumph of his dreams.

The forests, with their myriad tongues,
    Shouted of liberty ;
And the Blast of the Desert cried aloud,
    With a voice so wild and free,
That he started in his sleep and smiled
    At their tempestuous glee.

He did not feel the driver's whip,
   Nor the burning heat of day ;
For Death had illumined the Land of Sleep,
   And his lifeless body lay
A worn-out fetter, that the soul
   Had broken and thrown away !

THE GOOD PART,

THAT SHALL NOT BE TAKEN AWAY.

SHE dwells by Great Kennawa's side,
　　In valleys green and cool ;
And all her hope and all her pride
　　Are in the village school.

Her soul, like the transparent air
　　That robes the hills above,
Though not of earth, encircles there
　　All things with arms of love.

And thus she walks among her girls
　　With praise and mild rebukes !
Subduing e'en rude village churls
　　By her angelic looks.

She reads to them at eventide
　　Of One who came to save ;
To cast the captive's chains aside,
　　And liberate the slave.

228

And oft the blessed time foretels
    When all men shall be free;
And musical, as silver bells,
    Their falling chains shall be.

And following her beloved Lord
    In decent poverty,
She makes her life one sweet record
    And deed of charity.

For she was rich, and gave up all
    To break the iron bands
Of those who waited in her hall,
    And labored in her lands.

Long since beyond the Southern Sea
    Their outbound sails have sped,
While she, in meek humility,
    Now earns her daily bread.

It is their prayers, which never cease
    That clothe her with such grace;
Their blessing is the light of peace
    That shines upon her face.

THE SLAVE IN THE DISMAL SWAMP.

In dark fens of the Dismal Swamp
   The hunted Negro lay ;
He saw the fire of the midnight camp,
And heard at times a horse's tramp
   And a bloodhound's distant bay.

Where will-o'-the wisps and glowworms
     shine,
   In bulrush and in brake ;
Where waving mosses shroud the pine,
And the cedar grows, and the poisonous vine
   Is spotted like the snake ;

Where hardly a human foot could pass,
   Or a human heart would dare,
On the quaking turf of the green morass
He crouched in the rank and tangled grass
   Like a wild beast in his lair.

A poor old slave, infirm and lame ;
   Great scars deformed his face ;

On his forehead he bore the brand of shame,
And the rags, that hid his mangled frame,
   Were the livery of disgrace.

All things above were bright and fair,
   All things were glad and free ;
Lithe squirrels darted here and there,
And wild birds filled the echoing air
   With songs of Liberty !

On him alone was the doom of pain,
   From the morning of his birth ;
On him alone the curse of Cain
Fell, like a flail on the garnered grain,
   And struck him to the earth !

THE SLAVE SINGING AT MIDNIGHT.

Loud he sang the psalm of David !
He, a Negro and enslaved,
Sang of Israel's victory,
Sang of Zion, bright and free.

In that hour, when night is calmest,
Sang he from the Hebrew Psalmist,
In a voice so sweet and clear
That I could not choose but hear.

Songs of triumph, and ascriptions,
Such as reached the swart Egyptians,
When upon the Red Sea coast
Perished Pharaoh and his host.

And the voice of his devotion
Filled my soul with strange emotion ;
For its tones by turns were glad,
Sweetly solemn, wildly sad.

Paul and Silas, in their prison,
Sang of Christ, the Lord arisen,

And an earthquake's arm of might
Broke their dungeon-gates at night.

But, alas ! what holy angel
Brings the Slave this glad evangel?
And what earthquake's arm of might
Breaks his dungeon-gates at night?

THE WITNESSES.

In Ocean's wide domains
    Half buried in the sands,
Lie skeletons in chains,
    With shackled feet and hands.

Beyond the fall of dews,
    Deeper than plummet lies,
Float ships, with all their crews,
    No more to sink or rise.

There the black Slave-ship swims,
    Freighted with human forms,
Whose fettered, fleshless limbs,
    Are not the sport of storms.

These are the bones of Slaves;
    They gleam from the abyss;
They cry, from yawning waves,
    "We are the Witnesses!"

Within Earth's wide domains
    Are markets for men's lives;

Their necks are galled with chains,
    Their wrists are cramped with **gyves.**

Dead bodies, that the kite
    In deserts makes its prey ;
Murders, that with affright
    Scare schoolboys from their **play !**

All evil thoughts and deeds ;
    Anger, and lust, and pride ;
The foulest, rankest weeds,
    That choke Life's groaning **tide !**

These are the woes of Slaves ;
    They glare from the abyss ;
They cry, from unknown graves,
    "We are the Witnesses !"

THE QUADROON GIRL.

THE Slaver in the broad lagoon
　　Lay moored with idle sail ;
He waited for the rising moon,
　　And for the evening gale.

Under the shore his boat was tied,
　　And all her listless crew
Watched the gray alligator slide
　　Into the still bayou.

Odors of orange-flowers, and spice,
　　Reached them from time to time,
Like airs that breathe from Paradise
　　Upon a world of crime.

The Planter, under his roof of thatch,
　　Smoked thoughtfully and slow ;
The Slaver's thumb was on the latch,
　　He seemed in haste to go.

He said, "My ship at anchor rides
　　In yonder broad lagoon ;

I only wait the evening tides,
  And the rising of the moon."

Before them, with her face upraised,
  In timid attitude,
Like one half curious, half amazed,
  A Quadroon maiden stood.

Her eyes were, like a falcon's, gray,
  Her arms and neck were bare ;
No garment she wore save a kirtle gay,
  And her own long, raven hair.

And on her lips there played a smile
  As holy, meek, and faint,
As light in some cathedral aisle
  The features of a saint.

"The soil is barren,—the farm is old ; "
  The thoughtful Planter said ;
Then looked upon the Slaver's gold,
  And then upon the maid.

His heart within him was at strife
  With such accursed gains ;
For he knew whose passions gave her life,
  Whose blood ran in her veins.

But the voice of nature was too weak;
   He took the glittering gold !
Then pale as death grew the maiden's
   cheek,
Her hands as icy cold.

The Slaver led her from the door,
   He led her by the hand,
To be his slave and paramour
   In a strange and distant land !

THE WARNING.

Beware! The Israelite of old, who tore
  The lion in his path,—when poor, and
    blind,
He saw the blessed light of heaven no more,
  Shorn of his noble strength and forced to
    grind
In prison, and at last led forth to be
A pander to Philistine revelry,—

Upon the pillars of the temple laid
  His desperate hands, and in its overthrow
Destroyed himself, and with him those who
    made
  A cruel mockery of his sightless woe ;
The poor, blind Slave, the scoff and jest of
    all,
Expired, and thousands perished in the fall !

There is a poor, blind Samson in this land,
  Shorn of his strength, and bound in bonds
    of steel,

Who may, in some grim revel, raise his
    hand,
  And shake the pillars of this Common-
    weal,
Till the vast Temple of our liberties
A shapeless mass of wreck and rubbish lies